LECTURES AND ADDRESSES.

LECTURES AND ADDRESSES

ON

LITERARY AND SOCIAL TOPICS.

BY THE LATE

Rev. FREDERICK W. ROBERTSON, M.A.,

OF BRIGHTON.

BOSTON:

TICKNOR AND FIELDS.

M DCCC LIX.

RIVERSIDE, CAMBRIDGE:
STEREOTYPED BY H. O. HOUGHTON AND COMPANY.

THURSTON AND TORRY, PRINTERS.

TO

WORKING MEN,

AND ESPECIALLY TO THE

WORKING MEN OF BRIGHTON,

THIS VOLUME,

CONTAINING SO MANY OF THEIR FRIEND'S UTTERANCES

IN THEIR BEHALF,

IS CORDIALLY DEDICATED.

CONTENTS.

PREFACE.

This volume consists of Lectures and Addresses delivered by the late Rev. Frederick W. Robertson before the members of the Working Man's Institute, or of the Athenæum at Brighton, to which have been added some Speeches delivered on occasions of public interest.

It may be fitting, by way of Preface to these Addresses, some of which have been published before in separate forms, to give a brief account of the circumstances attending their delivery. A few letters have been added as bearing directly on the subjects.

The first was the opening address of the Working Man's Institute at Brighton, in 1848. This Institution mainly owed its origin to the late Mr. Holtham, who, having always felt a warm interest in the progress of the working classes, elaborated, during a severe illness, a plan of a Literary Institute, which was to be governed entirely by the working men. They were to owe no part of their management to the patronage or assistance of their richer neighbours, although they were willing that such should contribute to the funds of the Institution, and even become honorary members.

The Committee were very desirous that Mr. Robertson should open the Institute with an Address, and accordingly Mr. Holtham, the President, wrote to him on the subject. In reply he says:—

"I do not think I am at all the man that should be selected. They should have some one of standing and influence in the town, and I am almost a stranger; and my taking so prominent a position might fairly be construed into assumption. Again, I am much afraid that my name might do them harm rather than good. They wish not to be identified at all with party politics and party religion; and I fear that in the minds of very many of the more influential inhabitants of the town, my name being made conspicuous, would be a suspicious circumstance. It is my conviction that an address from me would damage their cause. For though the Institution is intended to be self-supporting, yet there is no reason why it should wilfully throw away its chances of assistance from the richer classes, and I am quite sure that of these very many, whether reasonably or unreasonably, are prejudiced against me; and perhaps the professedly religious portion of society most strongly so. Now I do think this is a point for very serious consideration, and I think it ought to be distinctly suggested to the Committee before I can be in a position to comply with or decline complying with their request.

"Besides this, I believe that they have erred in the estimate of mental calibre. I wish most earnestly for their own sakes that they would select a better man."

Subsequently he writes as follows:—

"Last night I attended the meeting of the Working Man's Institute, and was very much struck with the genuine, manly, moral tone of the speakers. I went home with quite elevated hopes for my country, when I compared the tone with that of the French clubs. And my whole heart sympathized with what your feelings must have been in the success of your brave efforts. Of course people who expect in it a perfect Utopia will be disappointed, or gratified, by finding it *so far* a failure. But the similar institutions of the upper classes have been, like all human things, checkered with good and evil; a means of increasing the powers of good men for good, and those of bad men for bad. You do not expect more than this; the inevitable result of all powers and privileges added to humanity. But they *must* be added, come what may. There is no other intelligible principle which will not be compelled in consistency to recognize barbarism as the highest state."

Writing to Lady Henley at this time, Mr. Robertson says:—

"I am anxious to enlist your sympathy in the cause which I am trying to assist. The case is this. About 1,100 working men in this town have just organized themselves into an association which, by a small weekly subscription, enables them to have a library and reading-room. Their proceedings hitherto have been marked by singular judgment and caution, except in one point, that they have unexpectedly applied to me to give them an opening address.

"A large number of these are intelligent Chartists, and there is some misgiving in a few minds as to what will be the result of this movement, and some suspicion of its being only a political engine. The address on Monday is therefore expected to contain a proposal for boiling down the Irish landlords and potting them, to support the poor this winter; and another, more democratic still, for barrelling and salting the aristocracy and the parsons, for home consumption in the poor-houses. But I must gravely assure you that this is premature. Nor do I think such a measure would be expedient yet.

"My reasons for being anxious about this effort are these—it will be made. The working men have as much right to a library and reading-room as the gentlemen at Folthorp's or the tradesmen at the Athenæum. The only question is whether it shall be met warmly on our parts, or with that coldness which deepens the suspicion, already rankling in the lower classes, that their superiors are willing for them to improve so long as they themselves are allowed to have the leading strings. I wish they had not asked me, as it puts me in an invidious position as a stranger in the town; and I begin to suspect that my reason for writing this long note was to exculpate myself from the charge of affecting prominence in the town.

"The selection of books for the library is a matter of very great importance, as I have become aware, since getting a little insight into the working of this Institute, of an amount of bitterness and jealousy, and hatred of things as they are, which I had not before suspected in its full extent. And people go on saying, 'Peace, peace, when there is no peace!'"

The address was delivered and created a great sensation amongst all classes. It was marked by extraordinary oratorical power, and evinced a faculty for addressing a popular assembly greater even than had been expected.

The original plan of the Working Man's Institute failed; doubtless because it was based on a selfish policy of class isolation, rather than on the broad principle of union one with another. Some of the elements of its weakness may be traced in the second address which Mr. Robertson delivered to the members of this body. The result of that address was a determination by the majority to construct an association on wiser principles, and during the progress of this work, the success of which was very much owing to the zeal and energy of the Secretary and the Committee, Mr. Robertson was ever ready with wise counsel and efficient help. His heart was deeply with the working men, and plans and efforts for their elevation occupied much of his thought. The following extracts from letters written at this period will show that he gave them no half-hearted or formal assistance.

"I will pledge myself, if your society is formed, and contains in it the elements of vitality, to give either an opening address, or a lecture before the close of this year.

"But it seems to me a matter of great importance that public attention should not be ostentatiously called again so soon to your efforts at self-restoration, so long as they are only efforts. If the Institute is needed, really craved and earnestly desired by the working men, they will enroll themselves in sufficient numbers to ensure its existence without the excitement of an address. If they would not without this, then I am sure that to attempt to secure their adhesion by such means would be very dangerous.

"On the former occasion nearly 700, in a fit of transient enthusiasm, joined themselves, I believe, and (out of about 1,300) withdrew directly after. If artificial means are necessary to preserve its existence, then the society will soon die a natural death; and we should be again covered with the shame of an abortive attempt. The cause of the working men cannot *afford* this. Better fail silently than make another public confession of incapacity.

"Now an address at present would draw the attention of the town. It would perhaps induce waverers to join, as all public excitement does; and it might secure immediate ready money. But these are trifles compared with the risk of the withdrawal of many soon after. And suppose that enough to support the society did not join?

"Let me propose therefore: Begin your society as soon and as quietly as possible; that is, as quietly as is consistent with that publicity which is necessary to acquaint the working men with the fact of a new association being in process of formation. If sufficient members do not present themselves, then the thing quietly dies away till a better opportunity; and be sure that no artificial excitement could have given it permanence, though it might have caused a premature abortive birth.

"After some months, if the association lives with internal strength, then we may try external aids. I, for my part, pledge myself as I have said. But the great lesson for us all in these days of puffing advertisements, is to learn to work silently and truly, and to leave self-advertisement and self-puffing to people who are on the verge of bankruptcy."

The Committee were anxious that Mr. Robertson should be the President of the New Association, and in answer to their application on this subject, he writes :—

"In reply to your letter of this day, I may briefly say that the idea of my accepting the Presidentship of the Institute is quite out of the question. I do not consider myself competent for such an office, nor am I sure that it would be to the advantage of the society. . . . . I believe I could assist the members more truly, at all events more independently, in a subordinate position. Prominence and power are things for which I have no taste.

"I am *very* anxious that there should be no second failure, but I think that the greatest wisdom and experience are needful to prevent it. . . . . The working men have shown that even a right-minded majority is unable to protect itself against a turbulent minority, without the introduction of other elements of society to support them—to *support*, not dictate; for I should be very sorry to see a majority of gentlemen on the committee. But they want some, of weight and wisdom, to fall back upon. And, indeed, this is the only true democratic principle to my mind—not an oligarchy of the poorest; but a fusion of ranks, with such weight allowed, under checks, as is due to superior means of acquiring information.

"What grieves me to the heart is to see distrust in the minds of working men of those wealthier than themselves; and nothing is more mischievous or unchristian than to gain popularity with them by fostering these feelings, and insinuating that the clergy and the religious and the rich are their enemies, or only espouse their cause for an end.

"I *must* not accept any high office; I am their friend, but

I want nothing from them—not even influence nor their praise. If I can do them even a little good, well; but for their sakes I must not take any thing which could leave on one of their minds the shadow of a shade of a suspicion of my motives."

Some months after, very urgent representations were made to Mr. Robertson as to the benefit the struggling Institution would receive by his assistance in a Lecture, and he then wrote as follows to the Secretary :—

"In reply to your communication of the 21st, which I only had last night after an absence from Brighton, I beg to say that after much consideration, I have come to the conclusion that it is my duty not to refuse the request made to me.

"I am very unfit at present for the excitement of addressing numbers; but knowing that the insufficiency will be pardoned, and feeling deep interest in the success of the working men, I shall not allow this to stand in the way.

"I was not aware that the name of the Institution was to be changed. Is not this virtually acknowledging that the former attempt was a failure, instead of the society being, as I believe it is, the old one purified by experience? Not knowing the reasons for the change, which perhaps are valid, at first sight I am inclined to regret it. There is much in names, especially when they are associated with recollections which can be appealed to, and when they adhere to a society through many shocks and changes. Besides, 'Working Man' is a noble title for any human being; a human being's right title. 'Mechanic' is a poor class title, like Agriculturist, Botanist, Sailor, &c. &c. Besides, it is not true as a designation for your society; a schoolmaster is not a mechanic, nor a retail dealer of any kind, yet many such are in the society. Ought you not, like good soldiers in a great cause, *to stand to your colours?*"

That Society is now working admirably and efficiently under the name of the Brighton Mechanics' Institute, on principles which Mr. Robertson considered to be more in accordance with sound views of social and political economy.

The "Two Lectures on the Influence of Poetry" were given in fulfilment of the pledge contained in the foregoing extracts from letters; and their delivery created a great sensation. To those who never heard Mr. Robertson speak, it may be interesting to learn that he was gifted with a voice of wonderful sweetness and power. So flexible and harmonious was it, that it gave expression to the finest tones of feeling; so thrilling, that it stirred men to the heart. His gesture was simple and quiet;—his whole soul so thoroughly absorbed in his subject that all was intensely real, natural, and earnest.

The following letter from the Earl of Carlisle, on some points referred to in the Lectures on Poetry, is given, partly for the sake of the criticism which it contains, and partly because it leads, naturally, to one from Mr. Robertson, which further illustrates his views on poetry :—

"I would not thank you for your most acceptable present till I had enjoyed the pleasure of making acquaintance with its contents. I have recognized in them all the high ability and the generous and delicate feeling which I could have expected.

"Upon one or two points of mere taste we may not wholly agree, but there is no part of what you inculcate with which I agree more fully than that in which you commend universality of taste. I have some doubts, for instance, about this, 'the best poetry demands study as severe as mathematics require.'

"I take, what appear to me to be the highest of human compositions, the Iliad and Macbeth, and I think they both are eminently intelligible without pain or effort. Perhaps I would give up Hamlet to you—not Othello.

"I think you rate Dr. Johnson's poetical powers too low.

"'Rest undisturbed within thy peaceful shrine,
Till angels wake thee with a note like thine.'

"I must not, however, indulge in mere prattle. Let me repay your kindness in the same coin, of however inferior value. I assure you, with all truth, that I look on some things I have said with more complacency, when I flatter myself that there is some identity of view between us."

His lordship accompanied his letter by a copy of his Lectures on Pope, and Mr. Robertson replied—

"I will not allow a post to pass without thanking you very gratefully for your kind present, and kinder note, the approval of which I feel to be very invigorating. I was very glad to find that there was not a syllable of the Lecture on Pope, which jarred with my estimate of him, which I a little feared. But the passage quoted from Warton, page 10, and another of your own, page 16, ''Twas not so much the pomp and prodigality of heaven,' etc. express, though with far more precision, exactly the reasons which I briefly alleged for ranking Pope in the second order, but, in that order, first. I congratulated myself much on perceiving so far this agreement, and in all the admiration which the lecture contains, I heartily concur.

"The passage, page 105, 'Heaven was made for those who had failed in this world,' struck me very forcibly several years ago, when I read it in a newspaper, and became a rich vein of thought in which I often quarried; especially when the sentence was interpreted by the Cross, which was failure, apparently.

"My sentence, 'The best poetry demands study as severe as mathematics require,' is very justly open to criticism; but more, I think, from the unfinished abruptness of the phraseology than from its real meaning. The best poetry has a sense which is level to the apprehension at once; not being obscure in expression, nor metaphysical or scholastic in thought; but then any one who had caught this meaning at the first glance would be greatly mistaken if he supposed that he had got all, or nearly all, it meant.

"The dewdrop that glitters on the end of every leaf after a shower is beautiful even to a child; but I suppose that to a Herschel, who knows that the lightning itself sleeps within it, and understands and feels all its mysterious connections with earth and sky and planets, it is suggestive of feeling of a far deeper beauty; and the very instances you allege, Macbeth and the Iliad, would substantiate what I *meant*, though not what I awkwardly perhaps seemed to say. Macbeth, all action, swift and hurried in its progress towards *dénouement*, is intelligible at once. But I spent myself many weeks upon it, and only began at last to feel that it was simple, *because* deep. Some exquisite and fine remarks of Mrs. Jameson on certain characters in it, and profounder ones of Coleridge on others, have brought out a meaning that we feel at once was *in it*, and not forced *upon it*. In the sense I meant, I should say Macbeth could not be understood, especially as a whole, except with hard study.

"I am very much tempted to accept the challenge of page 28, in the Lecture on Pope. 'I would beg any of the detractors of Pope to furnish me with another couple of lines from any author whatever, which encloses so much sublimity of meaning within such compressed limits, and such precise terms.'

"If it were not that the cartel is addressed only to Pope's *detractors*, I think I should allege that wonderful couplet of the Erd Geist in Faust—

> "'So schaff' ich am sausenden Webstuhl der Zeit
> Und wirke der Gottheit lebendiges Kleid;'

at least if I might interpret them by Psalm cii. 26, 27.

"In the graceful courtesy with which your lordship acknowledges that there is 'some identity of view between us,' I receive the best and most cheering reward that my little pamphlet has obtained."

The Lecture on Wordsworth was delivered before the members of the Athenæum, and was to have been followed by a second on the same subject; but Mr. Robertson's health was never afterwards equal to the exertion. This lecture has not had the advantage of his own corrections. He was criticized by the South Church Union Chronicle as teaching in it "Pantheism," and as unfairly attacking High Churchmen. To this he replied in the following letter:—

"In the columns of the *Brighton Guardian*, denominated the 'South Church Union Chronicle,' I see some strictures on certain expressions attributed to me in my Lecture upon Wordsworth. With the tone of the strictures, excepting one sentence which I regret,—not for my own sake, for it is untrue, but for the writer's sake, for it is rude and coarse—I can find no fault. The whole criticism, however, is based on a misconception. It proceeds on the assumption that I complained, with blame, that—

"'High Churchism regarded with peculiar reverence a sanctity as connected with certain places, times, acts, and persons,' &c.

"I did not use those words. That was not my definition of High Churchism; and to have condemned it as so defined would have contradicted my argument, for I was actually at the moment justifying Wordsworth, who is well known to have entertained such feelings. Had I so spoken, I should have condemned a feeling of the *relative* sanctity of such things; a feeling which I comprehend too entirely to have any inclination to interfere with.

"What I did say was as follows: 'The tendency of Pantheism is to see the godlike everywhere, the personal God nowhere. The tendency of High Churchism is to localize the personal Deity in certain consecrated places, called churches; certain consecrated times, called Sabbaths, fast days, and so forth; certain consecrated acts, sacramental and quasi-sacramental; certain consecrated persons, called priests.'

"I endeavoured to show that the *tendency* is not necessarily the error; and that there are High Churchmen, like Wordsworth, who recognize in such places, persons, and acts, a sanctity only relative and not intrinsic,—relative to the worshippers, without localizing or limiting Deity in or to the acts, times, or places; Pantheistic and High Church tendencies, each false alone, balancing each other in the particular case of such men.

"I have no intention of entering into controversy on this point; and I should, according to my hitherto invariable practice, have left both the misrepresentation and the criticism unnoticed, were it not that the words, as they stand, if used by me, would have evidenced an unworthy desire of turning aside from my subject to pander to the passions of my audience, and seeking a miserable popularity by an attempt to feed that theological rancour which is the most detestable phase of the religion of the day.

"I do not merely say that I was not guilty of this paltry work. I say it is simply impossible to me. To affirm, whatever may be taught by our savage polemics, whether Tractarian or Evangelical, that the new commandment is NOT this—'that ye hate one another'—and that discipleship to Christ is proved more by the intensity of love for good than by the vehemence of bitterness against error, is with me a desire too deep, too perpetual, and too unsatisfied, to have allowed the possibility of my joining, even for one moment, in the cowardly cry with which the terrors and the passions of the half-informed are lashed by platform rhetoric into hatred of High Churchmen."

And, as further elucidating his opinions on these subjects, the following extract from a letter which he wrote about this time will be of interest:—

"I gratefully accept your hint about the definition of High Churchmanship. I will modify what I said, to prevent misunderstanding. At the same time, as High Churchmanship, in the sense in which I was then speaking, is in my view an error, I must represent it in its most developed, not in its modified form, and as the exact opposite of Pantheism. All grand truth is the statement of two opposites, not a *via media* between them, nor either of them alone. I conceive Wordsworth to have held both; the Personality of the Eternal Being, and also his diffusion through space. Now I cannot conceal my conviction that it is the vice of High Churchism in its *tendency*, to exaggerate the former of these, by localizing Deity in acts, places, &c. It is the vice of Pantheism to hold the latter alone.

"When a High Churchman fully recognizes the latter, as Wordsworth did, I care little for any trifling exaggerations of the former, and I will always fight for him and maintain that his High Churchism has no radical error in it, even though his *expressions* may to my mind seem to predicate locality of Him much more than I should like to do it. But when he represents Personality as a limitation to Time, Space, Acts, &c., instead of recognizing it in three essential points, all metaphysical and supersensual, viz: Consciousness, Will, Character, then I must earnestly and firmly oppose High Churchism, and say that its tendency is to localize; and I must quote anxiously those texts which, taken alone, have a Pantheistic sound. 'Howbeit, the Most High dwelleth not in temples made with hands. Heaven is my throne; Earth is my footstool; what house will ye build for me,' &c.

"And indeed I do think that this is a very common and very dangerous tendency. I will modify my definition by saying it is the *tendency* of High Churchism. That it is not inseparable from it I showed by defending Wordsworth. High Churchism I hate. High Churchmen, many of them, I love, admire, and sympathize with."

The next in order in this volume is the Lecture delivered at the opening of a Reading Room at Hurstper-point, a village about eight miles from Brighton, and which lecture Mr. Robertson consented to deliver from motives of personal friendship.

A reporter was present, and a fair copy from his notes was given to Mr. Robertson. That fair copy cannot now be discovered, and as these notes, in his own handwriting, appear to be the original preparative sketch of his lecture, and are so exceedingly suggestive, it has been judged better to print them as they were found.

The friend at whose instance this Lecture was delivered writes :—

> " . . . although the language used by Mr. Robertson was much above the comprehension of the agricultural class of the village, whose life is more marked by its stern contentment than of much self-education through the medium of books, yet I am able to record that there was nevertheless such a charm about this lecture as to excite a considerable number of the audience to request its immediate publication."

The Speech, on the question of closing shops at an earlier hour, is printed from a transcript from the shorthand writer's notes, aided by such private memoranda as were available; it was not popular with the *employés*, partly, it is believed, from some little misconception. Mr. Robertson could never be a mere partizan, and his clear judgment saw that, however desirable and right was the object which the young men were striving to attain, there were difficulties to be overcome which it was not wisè to ignore; and also that there were two sides to the question, the arguments not being exhausted by denouncing all the masters who hesitated in making the concession, as mean, selfish, and tyrannical.

As delivered, it was a noble speech; it did not of course win the loudest cheers; but it aided the cause of the young men more effectually than some other speakers did, who raised a temporary enthusiasm by refusing to admit that there were any obstacles but such as were represented by covetousness.

The Speech on behalf of the Association for improving the Dwellings of the Working Classes, was remarkable on account of the bitterness which it produced in some minds, owing to the fearlessness with which Mr. Robertson treated the Sabbath question.

At the time of this meeting, the Crystal Palace at Sydenham was being erected, and it was currently reported that the Government had granted a Charter of Incorporation to the Company, with permission to open the building to the public on Sunday. The country was much disturbed thereat, and Brighton was not behind other places in petitioning and holding meetings. Sermons were preached, simultaneously, in *nearly* all the pulpits in the town, on the general question of the desecration of the Sabbath; thousands of tracts on the subject were distributed, and associations formed.

From this movement Mr. Robertson held aloof; he preached a sermon on the subject, which, to many minds, was most conclusive;* and in reference to the controversy, which had become (on one side) very bitter, he wrote to a friend:—

"As you will be here next week, I will not write you a volume, for nothing less would do. I preached on the subject on Sunday, satisfactorily to myself at least, a thing which has occurred to me but once or twice in all my ministry; so I am thoroughly prepared with an opinion on a matter I have well considered. I will say at present I am quite resolved to sign no petition. Dr. V.'s pamphlet does not go to the root of the matter. I agree with him in viewing the move, so far as it is an *avowed* innovation, with great jealousy, but I cannot ask for a State enactment to reimpose a law which Christianity has repealed, without yielding the very principle of Chris-

* This Sermon is published in the Second Series of Mr. Robertson's Sermons, and should be read by any one desirous of understanding Mr. Robertson's views on this question, as it is treated there more completely than it was possible to do in a letter. There is also a Sermon on the "Shadow and Substance of the Sabbath," in the First Series, which may be read with advantage.

tianity. Historically, the Lord's Day was not a transference of the Jewish Sabbath at all from one day to another. St. Paul, in Rom. xvi. 5, 6, speaks of a *religious non-observance* of the Sabbath; I cannot say or think that the Crystal Palace affair is a *religious* non-observance, believing it to be merely a lucrative speculation; nevertheless, I have nothing to do with that. The Sabbath is abrogated, and the observance of a Day of Rest is only a most wise human law now, not to be enforced by *penalties*. Besides, how dare we refuse a public concession to the poor man of a right of recreation which has been long assumed by the rich man with no protest or outcry from the clergy, who seem touched to the quick only when desecration, as they call it, is noisy and vulgar?"

His correspondent suggested, in answer, Bishop Horsley's critical treatment of the question, and to this letter he replied:—

"'Horsley's Sermons' I only vaguely remember. I am quite at ease on the subject. The critical disposal of this or that text would not alter my views. I am certain of the Genius and Spirit of Christianity; certain of St. Paul's *root thoughts*—far more certain than I can be of the correctness or incorrectness of any isolated interpretation; and I must reverse all my conceptions of Christianity—which is the Mind of CHRIST—before I can believe the Evangelico-Judaic theory; which is, that Mr. . . . may, without infringement of the 4th Commandment, drive his carriage to church twice every Sunday, but a poor man may not drive his cart;—that the four or five hours spent in the evening by a noble lord over venison, champagne, dessert, and coffee, are no desecration of the command; but the same number spent by an artisan over cheese and beer in a tea-garden, will bring down

God's judgment on the land. It is worse than absurd. It is the very spirit of that Pharisaism which our Lord rebuked so sternly. And then men get up on platforms as . . . did; and quietly assume that they are the religious, and that all who disagree, whether writers in the 'Times,' Sir R. Peel, or the 'sad exceptions,' of whom I was one, to which he alluded, are either neologians or hired writers! Better break a thousand sabbaths than lie and slander thus! But the sabbath of the Christian is the consecration of all time to God; of which the Jewish Sabbath was but the type and shadow; see Col. ii. 16, 17. Bishop Horsley's attempt to get over that verse is miserable, I remember.

"'Six hundred churches wanted.' Yes! but when shall we have different hours for service and different congregations in one church, say one for three congregations; and so save two thirds of the money spent on stone and brick, that it may be spent on the truer temple, human beings in whom God's Spirit dwells? They do this on the Continent, and with no inconvenience. Besides, the inconvenience and mutual giving way, would be all so much gain for Christian life, instead of an objection to the plan."

A member of his congregation wrote to him on this subject, and, as was his wont, he replied fully and frankly.*

The occasion on which the next speech was

* That letter is not given here lest it should swell this Introduction to an undue limit, but it will be printed in a volume of "Letters on Theological, Philosophical, and Social Questions," which is now preparing for the press. It will not be out of place here to request that any one who may have received letters from Mr. Robertson on any of these topics would be so kind as to send them to the Editor of Mr. Robertson's Lectures, care of Messrs. Smith, Elder and Co., London. The letters shall be immediately copied and returned.

delivered, was one of the most interesting ever seen in Brighton. One hundred young men of Mr. Robertson's congregation signed an address to him, expressive of their gratitude for his unwearied zeal in their behalf. They invited him to tea at the Town Hall. Many others were also present, but all were men. That evening is well remembered still. It presented some remarkable features. One of the young men, Mr. C. H. Evans, rose and presented the address, and in doing so spoke with great feeling and earnestness of the benefit which he and the others, for whom he was that evening the mouth-piece, had received from Mr. Robertson's teaching. He dwelt on the reconciling, harmonizing spirit Mr. Robertson had induced between rich and poor—between the strugglers in life and their lot. He reviewed the characteristics of Mr. Robertson's public ministry, and vindicated it from the charges which had recently been brought against it in the columns of a certain party journal; and having adverted to the altered state of feeling in the working classes of the town, which he attributed mainly to Mr. Robertson's efforts to bring about a union of classes, expressed an earnest hope that long—very long—might the town have the benefit of his talents and self-devotion.

All rose as he spoke. Mr. Robertson was

deeply moved. All felt that if there were many ministers like him, how far brighter would become the prospect of a kingdom of Heaven upon earth.

The last speech in this volume was delivered on the memorable occasion of the attempt of Pope Pius IX. to parcel out England into Ecclesiastical Dioceses under Romish bishops, with Cardinal Wiseman as the head of the new Hierarchy. Every one will remember how that attempt was received. From one end of England to the other, one unanimous voice arose, "We will have nothing to do with Rome!" One of the largest meetings ever held at Brighton came together on this occasion to protest against this impertinent intrusion. All sects, all classes, met here on common ground—a stern determination that, whatever foreign despots might succeed in imposing on *their* peoples, Englishmen were determined never again to wear the yoke of priestly tyranny, least of all, the tyranny of Rome. It will be observed that the ground Mr. Robertson took was somewhat broader than that generally occupied. He rested his opposition to the Pope's decree on the inalienable rights of the individual conscience, in virtue of which it was not competent for any priest, or church, to dictate to men the terms of their belief.

Probably the controversy with Popery would be

more effectual, and more practical in its results, if the opinions which Mr. Robertson avowed were taken as the basis on which it should be conducted.

In former years, Mr. Robertson had delivered a Lecture at Cheltenham, on the Church of England's Independence of the Church of Rome; but it is omitted from this volume, because Mr. Robertson frequently expressed a very strong wish against its being reprinted, observing that his argument against the Church of Rome would now be based on altogether different grounds from those he had taken in that Lecture. Whatever weight may be attached to the critical rendering of certain texts—whatever authority may be claimed in virtue of certain canons or decrees of councils—the great principle that the conscience of each individual man is free to judge the Right, and to act in conformity with that judgment, without any interference or hinderance from any man or set of men—will be found to oppose a firmer barrier than these to Romish progress. The spread of Romish doctrine is simply impossible where this great principle of spiritual freedom is believed and obeyed.

It is very noteworthy, that nearly all these public efforts of Mr. Robertson were in behalf of those engaged in labour. He had a high idea of

Work, regarding it as God's appointment for every man; and while he always avowed his belief that the men of thought were labourers, as much as the men of action, he never lost an opportunity of urging on his hearers that a mere life of pleasure or of fashion—the life of busy idleness—was little better than living death. Some of his noblest utterances were those in which he sought to rouse men up to doing something better worthy of the vocation by which they were called. His own life was one long labour, of which, while others were marvelling at the wonderful gifts and graces it displayed, his own thought ever seemed to be "not as though I had attained." How little he esteemed the gifts which others valued so highly in him, may be gathered from a passage in a letter to a friend, written towards the end of his career. He says—

"If you knew how sick at heart I am with the whole work of '*parle-ment*,' 'talkee,' 'palaver,' or whatever it is called—how lightly I hold the 'gift of the gab'—how grand and divine the Realm of Silence appears to me in comparison—how humiliated and degraded to the dust I have felt, in perceiving myself quietly taken by gods and men for the popular preacher of a fashionable watering-place—how slight the power seems to me to be given by it of winning souls—and how sternly I have kept my tongue from saying a syllable or a sentence, in pulpit or on platform, *because* it would be popular" . . .

When many of the clergy and richer classes

were looking suspiciously at the growing intelligence of working men, and connecting it with revolutionary events then going on in Europe, Mr. Robertson threw himself boldly into their cause, and avowed his belief that they had rights which, if trampled on, it was at the peril of the social fabric; that they had wrongs which it were well for England if she recognized and set herself steadily to remedy. In public and private he ever sought to bring classes together.

His pulpit ministrations were chiefly addressed to the richer classes of society, and he never failed to warn them, with a stern yet loving faithfulness, respecting the special responsibilities and temptations to which they were exposed. Most unflinchingly did he seek to impress upon them the duties they owed to those below them in the social scale; * while, in speaking to labouring men, he as faithfully told them that one great cause why they were depressed and degraded was to be found in themselves; that when they could exercise self-denial, temperance, steadfastness in self-improvement, it would be simply impossible for any one to keep them down. He told them, too, that in obtaining the mastery over self, they were attaining in God's kingdom a rank and a

* See "The Church's Message to Men of Wealth;" published in the First Series of his Sermons.

nobility greater than any mere earthly title could confer. And both classes responded to his earnest zeal for their welfare, with a genuine love, which is very touching, very refreshing, in a day of conventional flattery and mutual self-laudation. Amongst many illustrations of the feelings of the Working Classes towards him may be mentioned this one. A pair of candlesticks was sent to him, accompanied by a letter, of which the following is a copy :—

"SIR,—A humble individual, desirous of acknowledging the *unflinching* kindness you have shown towards the working classes of this town, begs the acceptance of the enclosed; and, in doing so, he hopes you will pardon what I am afraid you will think an un-English way of sending a note without a name. My apology must be, that as you do not know me, you will not put any wrong construction as to my motive in doing so.

"Nothing but the profoundest respect would have induced me to take the liberty I have.

"Believing you to be a *man* as well as a gentleman, that you can come down to the level of working men, and *understand* them (a rare qualification now-a-days in one in the class that circumstances has placed you), all working men think it so much the more valuable to have your advice and assistance. May it long be continued.

"I do not complain that we have not the sympathy of the upper classes. I believe we have; but there is not one in fifty that can come down to our circumstances, to the bond of our common nature, to comprehend that, although the mechanic and artisan of this country are deep thinkers, yet they often stand in need of advice, and the assistance that education gives. We have their good wishes and pecuniary assistance—thanks for it, but sometimes a little kindly advice would do far more. It is this difference that makes us feel we could grasp you by the hand as a brother in the cause of progress of the nation. Would that there were more such. How much more would true religion, morals, and sound intellect be brought out. No fear then of the pope or the devil. Believe me, sir, I am very respectfully yours."

* * * * *

Referring to this letter, of which he never knew the writer, Mr. Robertson writes to Lady Henley :—

"You are quite welcome to copy that note; it does more honour to the writer than to the receiver; but except in cases where you can trust discretion, it would be better not to give my name. Ninety-nine out of a hundred would put my showing it you down to the score of vanity. You can show it, if you like, as a proof of the good and generous feeling sometimes found in lower life; but as there are many who hate me as a heretic, pray do not let them have a handle."

It will not surprise any one who knows human nature, to hear that, while to many people Mr. Robertson's teaching came like light in a dark place, to some it seemed revolutionary in politics, and heretical in creed.

Some influential persons spoke strongly against his teaching and his influence—it is believed with but very little personal knowledge of either; one went so far as to warn an attendant on the afternoon service at Trinity Chapel that if that attendance should be continued, the light of his countenance would be withdrawn; and this threat, which would have been disregarded so far as personal consequences were to be feared, became operative when the consideration of the consequences of such withdrawal to dear relatives was pressed and considered.

Some persons talked of "Neology;" and an active platform orator, well known at Exeter Hall, was brought down to deliver two lectures on "Neologianism." It was well understood by Mr. Robertson's congregation, that it was as a protest against their pastor that this was done. There are those who still remember the extreme perplexity of some excellent people who, recognizing in the names advertised to attend the meeting those clergymen whom they had been accustomed always to feel quite safe and comfortable in sitting under, were notwithstanding much confused by the new word, and anxiously inquired what the lecture was about. Was it a religious meeting? or a scientific meeting? or what was it?

Well, the lectures were delivered, and it is no disparagement to the zeal of the reverend orator to say that Trinity Chapel continued just as full, and

Mr. Robertson's influence just as great, as before these gratuitous lectures on "Neologianism."

It is gratifying to be able to record that he against whom these and other similar demonstrations were made—some, by the way, not quite so manly and open as this—was in no way disturbed nor annoyed by them. Never did an angry word pass his lips respecting any of those whom he knew were branding him as a heretic—who were trying, as far as they could, to hinder his ministry, or discredit him in the so-called religious world.

Towards the close of his ministry, it became evident that the only chance of his restoration to health was by having rest, and his congregation raised a fund for the payment of a curate; of course leaving the selection of the curate to Mr. Robertson. In a letter written at this time he says:—

"One inducement towards accepting their offer is, that it would enable me to take a district, and try to work it, with a view to physical, as well as spiritual, improvement of the poor; acknowledging Christ as the 'Saviour of the body;' a truth ingeniously ignored."

And writing on the same subject a little later, he says:—

"I am anxious, on my own account, for assistance, in order

to enable me to devote myself less exclusively to pulpit work, and to become more pastoral."

No curate came, however, to Trinity Chapel. It is not proposed in this place to enter on the question how it was that the plan was frustrated, —a more fitting occasion will present itself.

Mr. Robertson felt this acutely, and says of it, in writing to a friend,—

"I am deeply disappointed; I have looked forward to friendly coöperation and leisure for pastoral work. *Dîs aliter visum:* an old heathen adage to be translated silently into Christian phraseology; but right enough, and pious in feeling."

Those who were with Mr. Robertson at this time, remember well the utter self-forgetfulness which characterized his words and actions in relation to this disappointment. Three months afterwards, Mr. Robertson was carried to his grave; with such marks of respect, and reverence, and love, as perhaps never before accompanied a public funeral.

The family intended the funeral to have been strictly private; but when vast numbers signified their intention of accompanying his mortal remains to their last resting-place, it became evident that it would really be a demonstration of general mourning. The shops were closed, the houses shut up, and the presence of sorrowing thousands told more eloquently than words could do, what grief was felt at the loss Brighton had sustained. Foremost in this genuine expression of feeling were the working men of the town—the men he was proud to call "My friends—the working classes."

November 15, 1858.

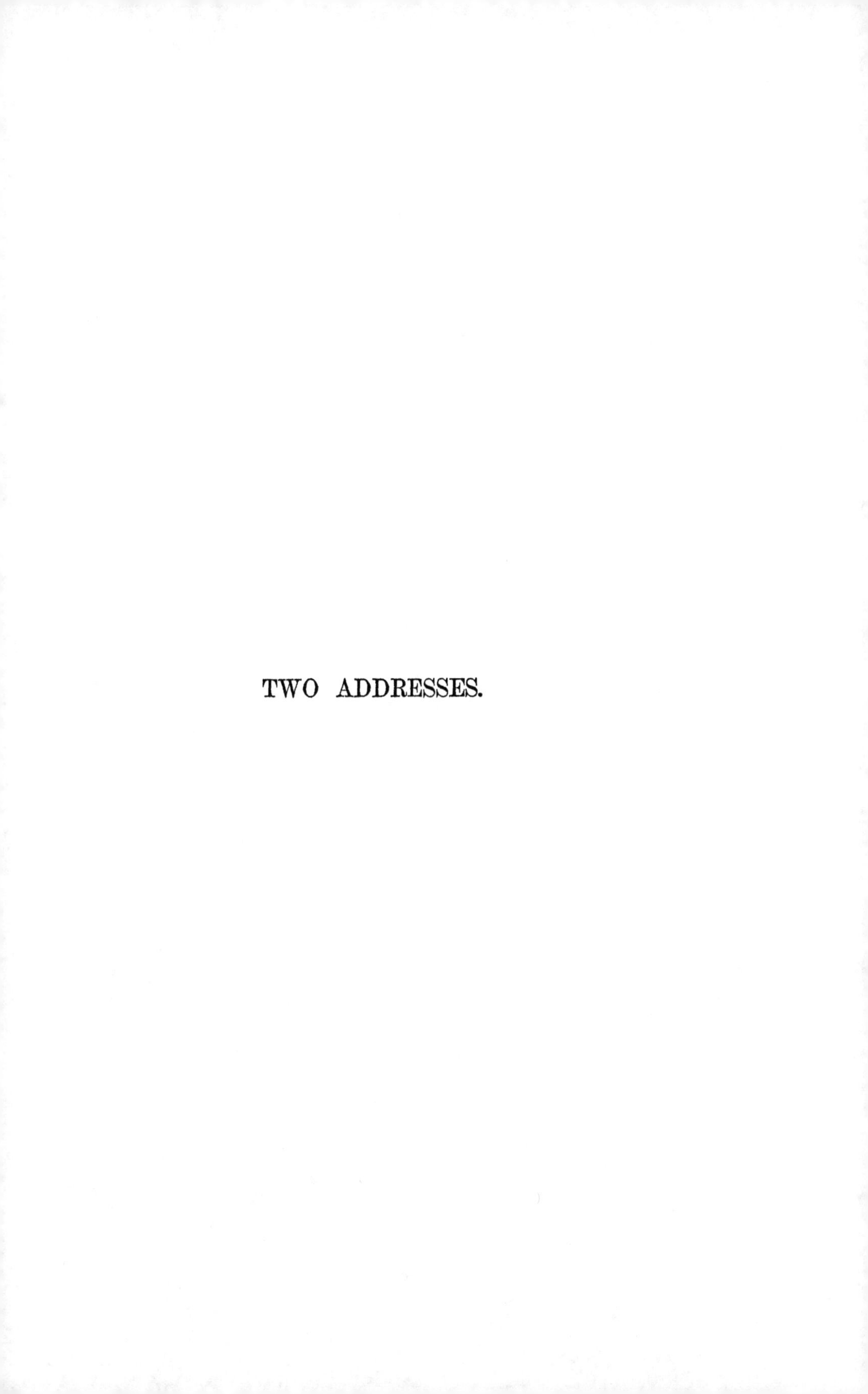

TWO ADDRESSES.

LECTURES AND ADDRESSES.

An Address delivered at the Opening of the Working Men's Institute, on Monday, October* 23, 1848.

Brother Men and Fellow Townsmen,

I owe it to you and I owe it to myself to give some explanation of my being here to-night to deliver an opening address to the Working Men's Institute. I owe it to you, or rather, to some of you, since it is only a few weeks ago that, on the plea of ill health, I professed myself unable to deliver a lecture to the Brighton Athe-

* A third edition of this Pamphlet having been called for, I have sent it to the press unaltered; for though the Working Men's Institute, owing to certain errors in the details of its organization, has for the present ended in partial failure, yet the very circumstances of its history have only confirmed me more than ever in the principles which it was attempted to express in the following pages.—F. W. R., *Oct.* 1850.

næum. Almost immediately after that I accepted your invitation, in which there is an apparent inconsistency. I owe it to myself, because there will lie against me in the judgment of many a charge of presumption. I have been in this town but a single year. I am but a stranger here. For one without name, without influence, without authority, without talent, to occupy a position so prominent as that which I occupy to-night, would really seem to justify a suspicion of something like vanity and assumption.

My reasons for undertaking this office are these: I did it partly on personal grounds. It would be affectation to deny that the spontaneous request of a body of men, delegated by a thousand of my fellow townsmen, is a source of very great satisfaction. It gave me great pleasure, at the same time that it deeply humbled me. I earnestly wish I were more worthy of the confidence reposed in me. My second reason for standing before you to-night is a public one. It seems to me a significant circumstance that your request was made to a clergyman of the Church of England. A minister of the Church of England occupies a very peculiar position. He stands, generally by birth, always by position, between the higher and lower ranks. He has free access to the mansion of the noble, and welcome in the cottage of the labourer. And if I understand aright the mission of a minister of the Church of England, his peculiar and sacred call is, to stand as a link of union between the two extremes of society; to demand of the highest in this land, with all respect but yet firmly, the performance of their duty to those beneath them; to soften down the asperities and to soothe the burning jealousies which are too often found rankling in the minds of those who, from a position full of wretchedness, look up with almost excusable bitterness on such as are surrounded with earthly comforts.

It seemed to me that such an opportunity was offered me to-night. The delivery of a lecture to the Brighton Athenæum on a literary subject was a secular duty, and one from which I felt I might fairly shrink on the valid plea of ill health; but the demand that you made upon me for this evening, though I urged it upon you that you had not selected the right man, was a sacred duty, which I felt it was impossible for me, on any merely personal grounds, to refuse. And if your call on a minister of the Church of England this evening may be taken as any exhibition of trust in the sympathy of those classes between whom and yourselves he stands as a kind of link,—if my acceptance of the call may be regarded as evincing a pledge of their sympathy towards you,—then, though all I say to-night may be weak and worthless, I shall not feel that I have spoken to you in vain, and to myself at least I shall stand acquitted of the charge of presumption.

I began to address you to-night by the name of brother men; I did not adopt the expression which my friend Mr. Holtham used in reference to your Committee. Yet, after all, we are at one. He did not mean to say that you are "gentlemen." He meant to say that you have, and that there was no reason why you should not have, the feelings of gentlemen. To say that a man is noble, does not mean that he is a nobleman. I do not call you gentlemen, because I respect you too much to call you what you are not. You are *not* gentlemen. To address an assembly of gentlemen by the title of "my lords," would be to insult them; and to address working men as "gentlemen," would be felt by you as an insult to your understanding.

The people of this country stand in danger from two classes; from those who fear them, and from those who flatter them. From those who fear them and would keep down their aspiring intelligence, they have no longer much to fear. The time is past for that; that cry of a wretched, narrow bigotry is almost unheard of now. But just in proportion as that danger has passed away, has the other danger increased, the danger from those who flatter them. From the platform and the press we now hear language of fulsome adulation, that ought to disgust the working men of this country. There has ever been, and ever will be found sycophancy on the side of power.

In former ages when power was on the side of the few, the flatterer was found in kings' houses. The balance of power is changed. It is now not in the hands of the few, but in the hands of the many. I say not that that is the best state conceivable; there might be a better than that. We would rather have power neither in the hands of the privileged few nor in the hands of the privileged many, but in the hands of the wisest and best. But this is the present fact, and every day is carrying the tide of power more strongly into the hands of the numbers; for which reason there will be ever found flatterers on the side of the many.

Now, whether a man flatters the many or the few, the flatterer is a despicable character. It matters not in what age he appears; change the century, you do not change the man. He who fawned upon the prince or upon the duke, had something of the reptile in his character; but he who fawns upon the masses in their day of power is only a reptile which has changed the direction of its crawling. He who in this nineteenth century echoes the cry that the voice of the people is the voice of God, is just the man who, if he had been born two thousand years ago, would have been the loudest and hoarsest in that cringing crowd of slaves who bowed before a prince invested with the delegated majesty of Rome, and cried, "It is the voice of a God, and not of a man." The man who can see no other source of law than the will of a majority, who can feel no everlasting law of right and wrong, which gives to all human laws their sanction and their meaning, and by which all laws, whether they express the will of many or of the few, must be tried—who does not feel that he, single and unsupported, is called upon by a mighty voice within him to resist every thing which comes to him claiming his allegiance as the expression of mere will, is exactly the man who, if he had lived seven centuries ago, would have stood on the sea sands beside the royal Dane, and tried to make him believe that his will gave law to the everlasting flood. For this reason I have not used this expression. I have not used it, because I would not flatter you even by an epithet. I respect you too much to flatter you. I used another title of address. For there are two bases of union on which men may be bound together. One is similarity of class, the other is identity of nature. The class feeling is a feeble bond; for he who feels awe for another man because he is in a rank above him, will cease to feel that awe if ever the man should cease to belong to that class. The pauperized aristocrat and the decayed merchant are soon neglected by their class. The man who respects another because he is in the same rank as himself, may cease to feel respect in one of two ways,—either by his own elevation, in which case he tries to keep the distinction broad between himself and the class that he has left, or else by the depression of that other man, through any misfortune.

Now, there is another and a broader bond of union to be found in identity of nature. When all external differences have passed away, one element remains intact, unchanged, the everlasting basis of our common nature,—the human soul by which we live. "We all are changed by slow degrees. All but the basis of the soul." Our tendencies to evil, our capacities of excellence are the same in all classes. It is just in proportion as men recognize this real, original identity of all human nature, that it is possible on this earth to attain the realization of human brotherhood. It is the only possible ground of union for the race. It was because this was not felt by the Jews of ancient times that they held themselves and their race proudly distinct from their Gentile brothers, and by that bigotry worked out their own inevitable downfall. The Christian of the middle ages tortured his Jew brother just because he did not recognize the same identity of sentiment and moral nature, which the great poet of our country has put so passionately and so touchingly into the lips of Shylock. "Hath not a Jew eyes? hath not a Jew hands, organs, dimensions, senses, affections, passions? fed with the same food, hurt with the same weapons, subject to the same diseases, healed by the same means, warmed and cooled by the same winter and summer as a Christian?" Had the feudal lord believed this he would not have put an iron collar round his serf's neck, nor made one law for the serf and another for the free-born. In our own times, if men who have been crying for the rights of our common humanity and the duties of our common brotherhood had understood the deep glorious meaning of their own cry, we should have heard nothing of those human tortures and that infernal cannibalism which have disgraced the cause of freedom. Get this deeply by heart, and all that is galling in artificial distinctions will pass away. Well do I know that this language I am using now respecting brotherhood and the equality of our human nature, is language that passes into cant. It has been defiled by cruelty; it has been polluted by selfishness; but we will not be ashamed of it for all that. In an age in which it has become suspicious, we will dare to believe in it and love it. It is buried deep in the eternal truth of things. That truth can no more pass away from the things that are, than heaven and earth can pass away. Sooner or later it must be realized in a more substantial form that it has yet ever assumed. All gradual improvements, all violent convulsions in the world are only doing their part in bringing this about. The thunder storm is terrible to look upon; but it leaves behind it a purer air and a serener sky. Let us hear the Ayrshire ploughman in his high prophetic strain:—

> "For a' that, and a' that,
> It's coming yet for a' that,
> That man to man the world o'er
> Shall brothers be for a' that."

Therefore it is that passing by all those abortive attempts which would fain produce a feeling of union by the false idea of similarity of class, I have fastened my attention on the real equality of our common nature, and called you "brother men."

In my address to-night, I propose to let its topics be suggested by the expressions of your own sentiments contained in the paper which your Committee put into my hand. That paper specifies the objects of your institution, and the spirit in which it has been established.

The objects of the Institution are two: it is intended to provide the working men of this town with the means of mental, and besides that, with the means of moral, improvement. Farther down I find mental improvement separated by you into two divisions. Mental improvement, you say, is the information of the intellect, and the elevation of the taste. You wish to inform the intellect. I confine myself to-night to one branch of this improvement, political information. I do it for several reasons. First of all, the means of acquiring knowledge which your Institution places in your hands are in a very preponderating degree of a political character. By works of history and the newspapers of the day, you will have that which will inform you of the constitution of your country.

My second reason for dwelling chiefly upon this branch of mental improvement is, that political science is the highest education that can be given to the human mind. Let me explain myself. When we in popular phraseology speak of politics, we ascribe to that word a narrow meaning. When we say that two men are talking politics, we often mean that they are wrangling about some mere party question. When I use the term "politics" this evening, I use it in the sense in which it was used by all the great and noble authors of the ancient world, who meant by the science of politics the intelligent comprehension of a man's position and relations as a member of a great nation. You will observe that in this sense politics subordinate to themselves every department of earthly science. A man who understands nothing of agriculture, nothing of trade, nothing of human nature, nothing of past history, nothing of the principles of law, cannot pretend to be more than a mere empiric in political legislation. Every thing that man can know is subservient to this noble science. Understood in this sense, the working men of this country have an interest in politics. For, in the first place, political ignorance is not a safe thing for this or any other country. The past is a proof of that. What was it but political ignorance which dictated a few years ago the letters signed "Swing," when the labouring men burned the hay rick and the corn stack in the wise expectation of bettering their own condition by that?

It needed very little political economy to teach them that all the wages in the world would not make a country rich, when its real resources are destroyed; that gold is but the symbol of another and a more real wealth for which it stands as the convenient expression; that the increase of their money would not give any increase in their comforts; and that when the country's means of subsistence are diminished all the coin in the country could not enrich them. What was it but political ignorance that suggested the workman's strike for wages? A very little political information would have told him that it is to a small extent that the master can regulate the wages he gives, that they depend on many things over which he has no control, as for instance, on the supply of labour in the market and on the demand for the commodity. Besides this, if there be a man in the country to whom politics are of personal consequence, it is the labouring man. A man in the higher classes may turn his attention to them, if he likes; nothing *forces* him to do so. It is to him a matter of amusement, a speculation—a theoretical curiosity—not necessarily any thing more. The difference of a penny in the price of a loaf makes no perceptible change on his table; but it may make the poor man's grate empty for a fortnight. If an unfair tax be imposed, a man in the upper ranks will scarcely be compelled to retrench a luxury in his establishment; but to the poor man it is almost a matter of life and death. Therefore a labouring man will be, must be a politician; he cannot help it; and the only question is, whether he shall be an informed one or an uninformed one. To him politics are a thing of daily feeling; but the man who feels a wrong most severely is not generally the man who is in the best state for calmly ascertaining the causes of the wrong. The child which feels the pin that pricks, knows better than any one can tell it that there is something wrong; but it is not exactly the one to judge when it strikes at random, whether it be the nurse's fault or the fault of circumstances. The uneducated man is precisely in the same position; he feels politically the sharpness and the torture of his position; but he is just as likely in his exasperation to raise his hand against an innocent government as against a guilty one. Therefore it was that in past times, when a pestilence came, the poorer classes, believing that it was caused by the medical men of the country for their own benefit, visited their fury upon them. They felt keenly, they struck wrongly. Tell us, then, whether it be safe and whether it be wise that the poor man, or that any class, should be profoundly ignorant of politics?

There is another reason, one more important still, for extending political knowledge. In this free country the labouring man has already a political responsibility. By degrees he will have, and ought to have, more. There is scarcely a man standing before me who has not something to do with the political government of his country. It may be that he has a vote in the vestry; or he is liable to be called on to serve on the jury, where he disposes of the life and liberty of his fellow-subjects; or perhaps he has a vote in the election of a member of parliament. The possession of that vote gives to the working man a solemn responsibility. Let us not be told that the injury done by a wrong vote is small; it is not so that we measure responsibility. If there be a million voters, and a man votes corruptly, it is true, it is but the millionth part of the injury which may arise from a bad law that is attributable to him; but responsibility is measured not by the amount of injury which results, but by the measure of distinctness with which the conscience has the opportunity of distinguishing between right and wrong. That man is not worthy of a vote in this country who gives his vote to the temptation of a bribe; neither is he worthy who bribes a man to vote against his conscience. That man is not worthy of a vote who intimidates another; nor is he worthy who suffers himself to be intimidated. That man misuses his privilege who corrupts by exclusive dealing; so does he who votes solely from self or class interest. For example, if the agriculturist voted for the retention of the corn laws because they enhanced the price of his corn, though he believed it would be to the injury of the rest of the community, that man was not worthy of a vote. On the other hand, if the manufacturer voted for the abolition of the corn laws, because he believed it would be good for the manufacturing interest, without considering how it would bear on the residue of the nation, that man exercised his vote wrongly; his vote was given him for the good of the nation, and he was sacrificing the whole of the nation to a part of it.

Now let me say another thing without offence. I scarcely know whether it is quite fair to say it on this occasion; but I feel perfectly confident that every honest supporter of the People's Charter will not misunderstand me. I will not say that that man is not worthy of a vote; but I will say, and I believe your feelings will only echo mine, that that man has not attained the true, lofty spirit of a British freeman who requires the protection of secrecy in his voting, who dares not risk the consequence of doing right, who has not manhood enough, except from behind the ballot box, to do his duty to his country and his God. Now to vote in this way, to vote incorruptibly, to vote on high motives, to vote on large principles, to vote bravely, requires a great amount of information. How far will the machinery of this Institution insure this? Only partially. We do not expect it will make the corrupt voter honest; it will not make the selfish voter liberal; but at least it offers the means of saving the honest voter from the consequences of his own ignorance, and of rescuing him from being the passive victim of the demagogue, or being compelled to throw his vote blindly into the hands of his landlord or his employer.

I pass to the second division of which you speak, the elevation of the taste. Taste is perception of beauty; to have taste is to recognize that which is right and congruous. When we speak of the moral sense, we mean the power of distinguishing between right and wrong; when we speak of taste, we mean the faculty of distinguishing that which is fitting from that which is unbecoming. There are many things which are neither right nor wrong, but which are yet offensive to good taste. It is not morally wrong to sit covered in the presence of a superior; but it is an offence against the propriety of manners. The juxtaposition of yellow and olive green is not a moral fault; but it is a fault to the eye which perceives the harmony of colours. There is nothing *wicked* in wearing a hat in a sacred building, or in discussing religious questions when the toast and the health are going round; but there is something which is exceedingly offensive to the feelings of religious propriety. The perception of all these harmonious fitnesses is what we denominate refinement, in contradistinction to vulgarity. But by vulgarity I do not mean the infringement of those laws which conventionality or fashion has laid down; for if fashion choose to decide that a man shall dine at seven, and he prefers instead to dine at one, though this may be a conventional, it is not a real vulgarism.

Vulgarity is quite distinct from nonconformity to arbitrary rules. We have sometimes met the deepest, truest refinement of heart in the man whose hands are black with labouring at the forge; we have met the greatest real vulgarity in the man whose manners wore a perfect outward polish, and who would never infringe the smallest rule of etiquette. In this sense do I speak of taste as a matter of importance to the working men of this country. What is it that prevents sympathy between class and class? Not merely difference of opinion, but difference of taste. The difference in feeling between educated and uneducated men places a great gulf between them. We are attracted and repelled by our instinctive sympathies even more than by our intellectual views. Let no one tell us that the workman cannot become refined; he is a refined man in foreign countries. Vulgarity is a thing almost exclusively English. Look at the poor Hindoo who goes through your streets asking alms. There is a grace even in his very attitude, an elegance in his address, which would almost make you believe it if you were told that he had been a prince in his own land. You may see, or might have seen, two peasants meeting on a high-road in France, and taking off their hats to each other with grave and dignified courtesy. The French peasant girl at a very trifling expense will dress herself in clothes that befit her station; but the inward refinement of her mind will be so reflected on the adjustment of every part of them, that she looks better dressed than the English lady's maid with all the aid of her mistress's cast-off finery.

There is another thing. The refinement of the workman's mind is a matter of importance in the works of art. Let any mercer place the silk that comes from Spitalfields beside that which comes from Lyons, and tell us if the one in point of elegance of design will bear any comparison with the other? Let the English watchmaker place his watch beside the delicate fabric of Geneva, or his clock beside that which comes from Paris, and tell us whether it be not rude and clumsy in comparison? Let the English china-maker place the manufactures of Worcestershire and Yorkshire on the same table with those of Sévres or of Dresden, and the superior beauty of the foreign article is visible at once. We are beaten out of the market whenever it comes to a question of taste. The reason is generally acknowledged to be this,—that on the continent the artist has freer access to that which is beautiful in taste and art. In the designs which adorn the Parisian clocks, you may trace the forms of beauty which existed originally in the minds of Raffaelle and Titian, and transfused themselves upon the work insensibly through every touch of one whose fancy had been inspired and kindled at the living sources of the beautiful.

A few years ago I was engaged in chamois hunting among the crags and glaciers of the Tyrol. My companion was a Tyrolese chamois hunter, a man, who in point of social position, might rank with an English labourer. I fear there would be a difficulty in England in making such a companionship pleasurable and easy to both parties; there would be a painful obsequiousness, or else an insolent familiarity on the one side, constraint on the other. In this case there was nothing of that sort. We walked together and ate together. He had all the independence of a man, but he knew the courtesy which was due to a stranger; and when we parted for the night, he took his leave with a politeness and dignity which would have done no discredit to the most finished gentleman. The reason, as it seemed to me, was that his character had been moulded by the sublimities of the forms of the outward nature amidst which he lived. It was impossible to see the clouds wreathing themselves in that strange wild way of theirs round the mountain crests, till the hills seemed to become awful things, instinct with life—it was impossible to walk, as we did sometimes, an hour or two before sunrise, and see the morning beams gilding with their pure light the grand, old peaks on the opposite side of the valley, while we ourselves were still in deepest shade, and look on that man with his rifle on his shoulder and his curling feather in his high green hat, his very exterior in harmony with all around him, and his calm eye resting on all that wondrous spectacle, without feeling that these things had had their part in making him what he was, and that you were in a country in which men were bound to be polished, bound to be more refined, almost bound to be better men than elsewhere.

Mr. Wordsworth, one of the great teachers of

our nation's feeling, has explained to us in many a passage how all these forms of God's outward world of beauty are intended to perform an office in the refinement of the heart. He has painted his country girl educated by the sky above her, the colours of the hills, the sound of the waterfalls—

> "Till beauty, born of murmuring sound,
> Shall pass into her face."

Now there are two things in your Institution which might educate taste of this kind: works of poetry and works of fiction. By poetry, we do not mean, simply, verse or rhyme. In a hundred thousand verses there might be not one thought of poetry. Neither does poetry mean something which is fanciful and unreal. By poetry we mean invisible truth as distinct from that which is visible. Not *every* invisible truth; not, for example, the invisible truths which are perceivable by the understanding, as mathematics; but the invisible realities which are recognized by the imagination. We will take an illustration. You look at this England, intersected with its railways, and say it is becoming a dull, prosaic thing. The sentimentalist will tell you it has broken up all the poetry of the scene, because it has run through our pleasure-grounds, sadly cut up our old retreats and solitudes, and destroyed all classical associations. So it may have done. It has destroyed that which was associated with the poetry of the past; but it has left us the real poetry of the present. Let men look upon that railroad, and one will see nothing but the machine that conveys the travellers to their destination. This is a truth, but only a visible one. The engineer comes and sees in it another class of truths. It suggests to his mind the idea of broad and narrow gauge, he talks of gradients, &c. Another truth; that which is appreciable by the understanding. Then let the poet come with that eye of his "glancing from heaven to earth, from earth to heaven," and his imagination creates another class of truths; the suggested meaning of it to him is the triumph of mind over matter; the gradual annihilation of time and space. He sees in these railroads stretched throughout the country the approaching times of peace and human union; and so he bursts out into his high prophetic song of the time—

"When the war drum throbs no more, and the battle flags
are furled,
In the parliament of man, the federation of the world."

All this is truth; neither seen, nor reasoned truth, but truth to the imagination. Truth just as real in its way, as the others are in theirs. And this is poetry. For this reason is poetry a thing needful for the working man. His whole life, if he could be taught to feel it, is full of deep, true poetry. The poet teaches him by suggestive inspiration the hidden meaning of common things, transfiguring life, as it were, by shedding a glory on it; and if you will force the poor man to see nothing but the wretched reality that is around him, if you will not let his mind be enlightened by the invisible truth of things, if you will not let him learn from the master thinkers of the past how in his work, in his smoky cabin, in his home affections, there is a deep significance concealed, connecting him, when he once has felt it, with the highest truths of the invisible world, you condemn the worker to a desolate lot indeed.

You have a second class of means in your Institution for refining taste,—works of fiction. It is in vain to rail at these with indiscriminate censure. Read they will be, and read they must be; and if we are asked the reason why works of fiction are matters of importance, the best reply which has been suggested is, that they enlarge the heart, enabling us to sympathize with the hearts of a larger circle of the human race than that into which our own experience admits us. You are all familiar with the works of Dickens.

The effect of that man's writings upon English feelings and English sympathies is quite incalculable. The peculiar feature of his works is, that their scenes are always placed in the ordinary walks of life. It is the character of all fiction now. The Clarissas and Grandisons of past ages have disappeared, and the life exhibited to us now is that of the lower classes of society. Men, who by reading the works of Cooper, had learned to feel that there was a real human life in the heart of the red Indian of the prairie, and who, by reading the works of Scott, learned that beneath the helmets and mail of iron which rust in our armouries, human passions and affections once beat warm, were insensibly taught by the works of Dickens to feel that in this country, close to their own homes, there was a truth of human life, the existence of which they had not suspected. We all remember the immense sensation those works made at first. If you asked the lady who was getting out of her coroneted carriage at the bookseller's shop what it was she wanted, you were told she had come to inquire if the new number of Dickens's last work were out yet. If you saw a soldier on the turnpike road with his knapsack on his back, reading as he went, and stepped up behind him, and looked over his shoulder, hoping perhaps to see that it was a tract, you saw it was the same everlasting Dickens. From the throne to the cottage this was true. What was the result of this? Imperceptibly, one which all the pulpits of the country would have been glad to combine in producing. The hearts of the rich and poor were felt to throb together. Men came to find that the rustic altar binds together two human hearts of man and woman with exactly the same feelings and anxieties and loves, as the marriage performed in the drawing-room, which united peers and peeresses. They discovered that when death enters into the poor man's hovel, it is just as much a rending asunder of a soul and body as if a spirit had been breathed away beneath a coverlet of silk. They came to find, too, that the lower classes have not a monopoly of all the simplicities of life, nor the upper classes the monopoly of all its absurd pride. People who lived in the highest ranks of life were startled to find that their own foolish jealousies had their exact repetition in the life which was going on beneath them. The ridiculous scorn with which the ancient family looks down upon the newly ennobled, and the newly ennobled looks down on the newly rich, has its exact counterpart in the sovereign contempt with which the small shopkeeper in his shop six feet square looks down on the poor apple-woman who has dared to bring her barrow too near the sacred neighbourhood of his aristocratic board. This was the achievement of these works of fiction. It was a lesson to us all, of humbleness, and sympathy, and mutual toleration; one step towards expanded love. And we can see no reason why such works should be injurious to the workman. We believe it is a narrow religion which scowls upon them all without discrimination. And the man of labour is free from one injury which arises to the man of leisure, from reading works of fiction. Works of fiction have in them an excitement for the feelings, in which one of their dangers lies. Every man has experienced how feelings which end in themselves, and do not express themselves in action, leave the heart debilitated. We get feeble and sickly in character when we feel keenly, and cannot do the things we feel. This is a great danger for the unoccupied and idle in the upper classes; but it is not possible that it should be so great a danger to the workman; his labour keeps him safe from it; so that it is perfectly possible for him, by reading works of fiction, to have his heart purified and refined by sympathy, at the same time that he gets something which is healthy and invigorating to counteract it in his hourly familiarity with the realities of toil and acting.

We come next to the moral improvement which you are anxious to effect. You explain this moral improvement to be "the elevation of the habits of the working man." You have, surely, begun at the right end. There are two ways of improving a nation's state; the one is by altering the institutions of the country, the other is by the reformation of its people's character. The one begins from things outward, and expects to effect a change in things inward; the other takes this line: from things inward to things outward. The latter is the right plan, and you have adopted it.

I believe I am addressing men of every shade of political opinion. There may be amongst us Tories, many of them men, of whom, whether they be right or wrong, this country has reason to be proud, for few other soils could produce them; men who felt that law is but an expression of a divine will, that the sovereign is the symbol of that will, and therefore in their way talked too about the divine right of kings, and believed most religiously that the happiness of this country depended on the connection of Church and State. I know that I address Whigs here to-night, of that party who gave the most distinct expression to their doctrines when, by our glorious Revolution, they stamped for ever on the constitution that great cardinal truth, that law is not the creature of the ruler, but that the ruler is the creature of, and owes his continuance to, the law. It is probable that I speak to Conservatives to-night, who, if we let them give their own account of their opinions, have seen in the teaching of all past history, that nations have had their seasons, infancy, manhood, and old age; and believing that England has reached the zenith of her manhood, are consistently opposed to all progress, because every step of progress seems to them a step towards decay. I may be speaking to Radicals to-night, who, if asked for the definition of their principles, would say, "Radicalism means root-work,—the uprooting of all falsehoods and abuses," and who would not hesitate in all solemnity of feeling to sanction their feelings by a divine principle, and take this text for their motto, —"Every plant which my heavenly Father hath not planted, shall be rooted up."

Lastly, I address men of another class altogether; who have felt burdens which crush the millions of the working classes with intolerable agony; and believing that only by throwing power into the hands of the majority, England's happiness can be secured, do therefore honourably and conscientiously build all their hopes on the People's Charter as the first step to be secured.

And whether I agree with their political views or not, I will never shrink from saying, in any society, that I am personally acquainted with Chartists, the integrity of whose purpose, the unselfishness of whose character, the firmness of whose principle is such, that if all resembled them, if all base men, whether high or low, could only be removed from the land, then the brightest day that England ever saw would be the day on which she got her universal suffrage; for universal suffrage would mean then only the united voices of all good men.

Now whichever of these views may be right, and I am not going to venture an opinion on that subject this evening,—whichever of these opinions may be right, there is a quackery in every one of them that pretends by the realization of itself, to give to this country all she needs. For instance, if a Tory gets what he wishes, a perfect loyalty, and his pattern kingdom should be only this, a tyrant sovereign, and a nation of slaves, I think he would say himself his toryism would do us no good. If the Conservative were to obtain his wish, "things as they are," and this were to leave us nothing but stagnation, moral, political, and intellectual, I think conservatism would do us no more good than toryism. If the Whig and the Radical were to realize their scheme, the entire overthrow of all abuses, the triumph of the sovereignty of law, and yet with that we got, as we might easily get, only a nation without reverence, and the abolition of old sacred associations, the heart of the country being left morally diseased and sick, whiggism would be as ineffectual as toryism or conservatism. Lastly, if the Chartist got all he wanted, universal suffrage, vote by ballot, equal electoral districts, annual parliaments, paid representatives, and no property qualification, and he should succeed in transferring all power into the people's hands, and yet it were to turn out that the majority were just as corrupt and depraved as the minority had been before them, every honest Chartist will tell us that his chartism would have been a failure, and was not worth the having.

Now the plan that you have adopted in this Institution seems to me to exactly reverse that order of procedure. You have said, "We will reform ourselves, and then the institutions will reform themselves." And in doing this you have surely proceeded in the rightful order; for if the heart of a nation be wise and right, you may depend upon it the laws of that nation will never long remain radically wrong. Free institutions will never of themselves make free men out of men who are themselves the slaves to vice; but free men will inevitably express their inward character in their outward institutions. The spirit of every kingdom must begin first "within you."

I now proceed to offer you two or three cautions with respect to your Institution. First, we must not expect too much from it. There is no magic, no enchantment, in a library and reading-room. They will not make a man wise or good in spite of himself, or without effort of his own. They will leave each man what he was before, except that they will put into his hands means of amelioration. The man who was the mere lounger in the streets will become the lounger in the Institute; the man who was the mere miserable politician there will remain the mere politician in the reading-room. The man who got excitement from drinking will now get excitement from the newspaper.

The next suggestion is, that we must be prepared for a great deal of evil. It is utterly impossible to look on this great movement without seeing clearly in the distance a large possibility of evil. The motto on one of your papers is, "Knowledge is power." It is a truth that is glorious, but at the same time terrible. Knowledge is power, power for good and evil. It is a power that may elevate a man by degrees up to an affinity with his Maker; it is a power that may bring him by degrees down to the level even of Satanic evil. Increased mental power will be the result of this plan—possibly that power will be devoted to bad purposes in many instances; it may become what it is not meant to be, the engine of some political party. Grant this. But are we to abstain from the granting of this power because of the possibility of its being turned to evil? Why, on that principle no good could be done at all. Good in this world cannot be done without evil. Evil is but the shadow that inseparably accompanies good. You may have a world without shadow; but it must be a world without light, a mere dim, twilight world. If you would deepen the intensity of the light, you must be content to bring into deeper blackness and more distinct and definite outline, the shade that accompanies it. He that feels timid at the spectral form of evil, is not the man to spread light. There is but one distinct rule that we can lay down for ourselves, and that is, to do the good that lies before us, and to leave the evil which is beyond our control, to take care of itself. In this world the tares and the wheat grow together, and all we have to do is to sow the wheat.

If you will increase the rate of travelling, the result will be an increase in the number of accidents and deaths; if you will have the printing press, you must give to wickedness an illimitable power of multiplying itself. If you will give Christianity to the world, He who knew what his own religion was, distinctly foresaw, and yet foreseeing, did not hesitate to do his work, that in giving to the world inward peace, it would bring with it the outward sword, and pour into the cup of human hatred, already brimming over, fresh elements of discord, religious bitterness, and theological asperity. Our path is clear. Possibilities of bad consequences must not stand in the way of this work. I see one thing clearly,—the labouring men in this town have a right to their reading-room and library just as much as the higher classes have a right to their clubs, and the middle classes to their Athenæums. Let no cowardly suspicion deter from generous sympathy. Give them their rights. Let the future take care of itself.

The other suggestion is this. Let not a public benefit become a domestic evil. In the upper classes it has been complained that the club has been the destruction of domestic comfort. It is easy for a man who has a few hundreds a year, by means of combination, to live at the rate of thousands. He may have his liveried servants, his splendid hall, his sumptuous entertainments, —and for this he may desert his home. The same may be one of the results of this plan of yours. But if a man wants an excuse to stay away from home, he will find it, whether this Institute exist or not. Moreover, it is not a comfortable, happy home that men will leave, but a home made wretched by a wife's slatternly conduct, the absence of cleanliness, the want of that cheerful, affectionate greeting which a man has a right to expect when he returns harassed and half maddened from the exhaustion of his daily work. Therefore, let there be a generous rivalry between your wives and daughters and this Institute. I tell them they have got now a rival. Let them try which has most attractions—a comfortable reading-room or a happy home.

I turn next to the spirit in which your undertaking has been carried on. I find in it two things, independence and generous reliance. You might have had an institution on a different principle. It is conceivable that some wealthy philanthropist might have provided you all this, at his own cost. You might have had a finer room, more brilliant lights, a better furnished library; but every man who entered that room would have felt his independence destroyed. He would have felt a kind of mental pauperism, getting his intellectual food at another's expense; and there is nothing that destroys all manhood so effectually as dependence upon the patronage of others. Now you have been independent. You have said, "We are men; we are not children; we will educate ourselves—it is our own duty." You have brought to bear the principle of combination. The subscription of one penny a week would go a very little way for one man. But a penny a week from 1,000 men amounts to more than 200*l.* at the end of a year. Enough, with a little assistance, for all you want. You have cleansed the building, washed it, papered it, furnished it, all with your own hands. Every man among you by this will in the first place feel independent; in the second place, he will have that elevation of character which arises from the feeling of property. Property calls out all the virtues of forethought, care, respect. The books, the furniture, all are yours. The sense of honest property in them will ensure that they shall be taken care of. Long may this spirit be characteristic of English working men. We can understand and honour the feelings of that man who stands before us with a modest feeling of his own dignity in his countenance, which seems to say, "The shoes that I wear are clouted, but I paid for the mending of them myself; the house that I live in is small, but every sixpence of the rent is paid for with my own money. It may be that my clothes are shabby and threadbare; but no man can say that the begging petition, except in case of the direst necessity, ever went round the town in my name." The greatest on earth has no right to look down on that man.

But not content with this, you have manifested the spirit of reliance upon others for their good will. There is one kind of independence which is akin to high excellence; another which is akin to restless, jealous pride. The former has been yours. Guarding yourselves against the idea of receiving charity, you have said to those who are better off than yourselves, "We will accept gratefully the books you choose to give us, we will thank you for your sympathy." Now let me say, with all the conviction of my heart, I believe that you have the sympathy of the upper classes. I stand not here to be the special pleader for the rich, or the defender of the vices of those around me. In other places I have spoken, I trust I ever shall speak, in their presence, in no sycophantic tone in the discharge of my duty. But now, in your presence, not for them, but for you to hear, it is but plain truth to say there is a deep feeling for you amongst them.

In these latter times a convulsion has shaken Europe, before which many a strong man's house built upon the sand has gone down. There has been a sifting of the nations; and every thing that had not the basis of reality to rest on has been shattered into shivers. Through all that terrible trial our own country has stood secure. The waves of revolution that thundered on distant shores, were only a feeble murmur here. The reason, politically speaking, of the difference is, that the upper classes in this country have hitherto been the leaders in reform. There are two ways in which alteration may be effected. If it be done gradually from above, it is a reformation; if suddenly from below, it is a revolution. If the higher do the work God has given them to do, of elevating those below, you have a country working out her own national life securely; if, on the other hand, those below either tear down wantonly, or by the selfishness and blindness of those above are *compelled* to tear down such as are socially their superiors, then there comes a crisis which no country ever yet has passed through without verging upon ruin.

England's reforms hitherto have begun from above. There was a time when the barons of this country, sword in hand, wrung from the most profligate of our monarchs the Great Charter of

English liberties. That charter imparted a portion of the freedom it won to the boroughs and the tenants, mediately and immediately holding from the Crown. When the insincere Charles I. came to the throne, who stood foremost in the resistance to the exaction of ship-money? An English gentleman by the side of an English peer. When his infatuated successor, with the blind arbitrariness of his race, untaught by all experience, began that system which ended in the expulsion of his family, the blood of freedom which flowed upon the scaffold, was the blood of an English nobleman. When that great measure passed which gave so large an extension of the franchise, it was proposed by a nobleman in his place, with a voice choked with emotion, produced by the magnitude of the change he was effecting. Come down to our own times. Who have busied themselves in insuring for the labouring man better ventilation, personal and domestic cleanliness? Who are they that, session after session, fought the battle of the working man to abridge his hours of labour? Who, after long and patient investigation, brought before the country the hideous particulars of women labouring harnessed in the mines, and children young in years but gray-headed in depravity? A band of English gentlemen, at the head of whom was one who has surrounded the name of Ashley with a glory, in comparison with which the concentrated lustre of all the coronets and crowns in Europe is a tinselled gewgaw, and which will burn brightly when they have passed into nothingness.

Another instance still. Suffer me to remind you of the history of your own Institute. At the beginning of this year a person of this town, afflicted with a severe malady, fixed his thoughts on this question, how he should do good to the working classes of Brighton. You may understand much of a man's real interest in a subject by observing the direction that his thoughts take when they are left to act spontaneously. A man who forces himself to think upon a generous topic does well; but a man whose thoughts turn to it of their own accord, when all coercion is taken off, loves that cause in reality. It was my privilege to visit this person during his illness, in my pastoral capacity, as a member of my own congregation. I found one thought uppermost in his mind, "How shall I do good to the working classes?" And that which was at first merely dim and vague, took form and shape at last. It grew, till it became a living thing; and whatever interest there may be in the crowded room now before us, whatever may be the result of this movement in your own intellectual elevation, whatever may be the future effects of it upon the minds of the men of Brighton, is all owing to the energy of one Christian philanthropist, who excogitated his idea in the midst of solitude, and matured it in torture. And that man is of a class above your own.

You have asked for sympathy. I say that you have it. I say not that the higher classes of this country have altogether understood the high destinies which they are called on to fulfil. I say not that they all, or any of them, do what they might. To say that would be to say what has been true of no country. There *are* nobles who see in their rank nothing of a higher call than that which gives them a miserable leadership in the world of fashion. There *are* land-owners who see in the possession of their land nothing more divine than the means of wringing rents from their tenants, and furnishing covert for their game. There *are* wealthy persons who speak of the workman as if he were of a different order of beings from themselves. The day is fast coming when they will find that their whole life has been a lie. After that the longer night is near, which will shroud all such in the darkness of all good men's scorn. But it is false to history—false to experience—false to fact, to give this as the general description of the upper classes of this country.

We pass to the last thing on which I have to speak to you. There is an expression in this paper of a hope "bright in the hearts of the labouring men that better times are coming." The heart of every one responds to that. Who can look on this entangled web of human affairs in which evil struggles with good, good gradually and slowly disengaging itself, without having a hope within him that there are better times to come? Who can see this evil world full of envy and injustice, and be content to believe that things will remain as they are, even to the end? Who can see the brilliancy of character already attained by individuals of our race, without feeling that there is a pledge in this that what has been done already in the individual will yet be accomplished in the nation and in the race?

If I did not respond with all my soul to that, I would close the Bible to-morrow. For from first to last the Bible tells of better times. It came to our first parents and spoke of the serpent Evil crushed, not without suffering, under the foot of man. It came to the Israelite, mourning under political degradation, and consoled him by the vision of a time in which kings shall reign in righteousness and princes shall rule in judgment. It came to true, brave men, who groaned over the hollowness and hypocrisy of all around them, the false glare and brilliancy which surrounded the great bad man, and told of the day when the vile man should be no longer called liberal, nor the churl bounteous. It spoke in the clearer language of New Testament promise of this actual world becoming a kingdom of peace and purity, of justice, brotherhood, and liberty. It irradiated the last moments of the first martyr with a vision of the Just One at the right hand of power.

Now suffer me to interpret for you the expression of "better times." If I understand you, you do not mean by "better times," times in which there shall be a general scramble for property; you do not mean the time when there shall be obliteration of all distinctions, no degradations for the worthless, no prizes for the best. You do not expect a time in which government shall so interfere to regulate labour that the idle and the industrious workman shall be placed upon a par, and that the man who is able to think out by his brain the thought which is true and beautiful, shall not be able to rise above the man who is scarcely above the level of the brute. Those would not be better times. They would be the return of the bad, old times of false coercion, and brute force.

But if I understand you aright, you expect a time when *merit shall find its level;* when all falsehoods and hypocrisies shall be consigned to contempt, and all imbecility degraded and deposed; when worth shall receive its true meaning, when it shall be interpreted by what a man is and not by what he has, nor by what his relations have been. You want the restitution of all things to reality. Those are better times.

Now, then, let us look at our England. Has she any part in these better times? They tell us that England's day is past. I have heard foreign philosophers dissect our political state, and, with cold-blooded triumph, by all the precedents of the past, anticipate our approaching fall. It may be so. In the history of the past, in the relics and ruins around us, there are the solemn monuments of nations once great that are now nothing. The land of the Pharaohs is in decay; its population is now diminishing, and the sand of the desert daily silting up the temples of her former magnificence; Rome is broken into fragments; Jerusalem's last sob is hushed. Spain once had an empire on which the sun never set, because the moment he set on her possessions in the east, he rose on her possessions in the west. Spain lies now in her hopeless struggle like the blackened hull of a vessel that has been lightning-struck, rolling and heaving helplessly as the ocean wills. Genoa, Venice, Holland, once had an eastern traffic. Upon them the same law of decay has passed, and the weed rots on the side of palaces that are now the abode of paupers.

It may be that such a destiny is in store for England. But one thing is certain, that the decay of morals in all these cases preceded the decay of institutions. The inward ruin preceded the political. So long as there was inward strength of constitution, so long intestine commotions were thrown off easily to the surface; so long as the nation was united in itself, so long were the attacks of enemies thrown off like the waves from the rock. To borrow a Scripture metaphor, if there were heard in the political heavens of a devoted nation or a devoted city the shrill shriek of the judgment eagles plunging for their prey, it was not till moral corruption had reduced the body of the nation to a carcase. Where the *body* was the eagles were gathered together. Looking to our beloved country, we see nothing of that kind. Her moral character seems yet sound. Healthy feeling is among us. A few weeks ago I stood in the lower room of this building, anxious to be a witness of the spirit in which you were conducting your undertaking. The speakers that evening, with one or two exceptions, were all working men. I heard, not eloquence, but something far better—straightforward, honest, English, manly common sense. A high moral tone pervaded all that was said. I heard vice decried. I heard lounging, drinking, smoking, all the evils that ruin the health and character of the artizan, sternly condemned. I trust that it did my heart good. And I hesitate not to say that I left that room with feelings enlarged in sympathy. I trod through the dark streets that evening with a more elastic step, and a lighter heart; I felt a distincter hope for this country—I felt proud of belonging to a nation whose labouring men could hold such a tone as that. Through all England we see the same thing; increasing moral earnestness, a deeper purpose, a more fixed resolve. Even in our justice do we see the same healthy tone. Justice is no longer the weak, passionate outbreak of vindictive feeling against a criminal for the injury he has done; in the very moment of her worst insult England can hold the sword suspended, and refuse to strike until she has maturely weighed not only what is due to the majesty of offended law, but besides, how much to the frailty of an erring judgment.

A striking exhibition of that same tone we have in the character of our press. On the whole, the press is on the side of rectitude. There is a paper familiar to us all, which is the representative of English humour. It is dedicated to mirth and jollity; but it is a significant feature of our times, and I believe a new one, that the comic satire of a country, expressed in a periodical, which tests a country's feeling because of its universal circulation, should be, on the whole, on the side of right. It takes the side of the oppressed; it is never bitter except against what at least seems unjust and insincere. It is rigidly correct in purity, distinctly saying in all this that England even in her hour of mirth is resolved to permit no encroachment on her moral tone.

Looking at all this, and seeing in the upper classes and the lower one strong feeling, one conviction that we have been too long two nations, one determination to become one, to burst the barriers that have kept us apart so long; looking at the exhibitions of high self-forgetfulness and sworn devotedness to duty, which from time to time are rising even out of the most luxurious and most voluptuous ranks, we have a right to hope that that which is working among us is not death, but life. Our national character is showing itself again in its ancient form, that strange character, so calm, so cold, so reserved outwardly, rising once again in its silent strength. The heart of England is waking to her work, that mighty heart which is so hard to rouse to strong emotion, but the pulses of which, when once roused, are like the ocean in its strength, sweeping all before it. This is not death. This is not decay. The sun of England's glory has not set. There is a bright, long day before her yet. There are better times coming.

SECOND ADDRESS.

PREFACE.

As this pamphlet may fall into the hands of some who are unacquainted with the circumstances which gave rise to its publication, and as some principles are involved in it which have a wider range than belongs to a local Institution, it may be well to preface it with so much information as may render it intelligible.

The Working Man's Institute was established in October, 1848. It was the belief of those who originated it, that a large class of persons were almost entirely destitute of any means of self-education by access to a library or periodical publications,—a class still more limited in means than those for whom Athenæums and Mechanics' Institutes had been long established. A very small subscription, one penny a week, if only sufficient numbers would combine, was found to be large enough to provide such an Association with the materials of mental and moral improvement; and it was confidently hoped that subscriptions from the wealthier classes would enable them by degrees to accumulate a valuable library. Great eagerness was manifested by the working classes when this project was made known. About 1,300 members enrolled themselves at once. The peculiar feature of the Association was, that the whole management virtually devolved upon this class alone, with the exception of one of a rank above them, the late Mr. Holtham, who gave up a large portion of his time to assisting in the organization of the Society; the object of this being to break down, if possible, that feeling of suspicion which exists in the minds of so many of the working class, of a desire for interference and coercion on the part of those who come forward as their benefactors.

It was, of course, foreseen that the rock on which such a plan might be wrecked, would be any successful effort to divert the funds and machinery of the Institute from its original intention to the purposes of a political party.

But in this case, the withdrawal of all well-disposed persons would leave the Association to dwindle till it became extinct. For its very existence depended upon numbers. The experiment, therefore, appeared to be a perfectly safe one, inasmuch as perversion of its purposes must inevitably be followed quickly by annihilation.

One fatal oversight (such at least it appears to the Author of these pages) in the constitution of the Society realized the foreseen danger. It had been justly held that the working men ought to have in their own hands the management of their own Society, lest the smallest suspicion should arise that there was any desire in those who were their benefactors to coerce or trammel them. Every attempt at interference was scrupulously avoided. All this was wise and just. But beyond this, not only was the domination of the upper classes made impossible, but even their assistance and advice excluded, by making honorary members incompetent to vote or act on committee; a mistake which originated in an over scrupulous generosity on the part of one who suggested it; but fatal, because false in principle.

To have vested the power of unlimited control or rule in the richer classes, would have been a surrender of the very principle on which the plan rested. But to reject all coöperation and assistance from them, to receive their contributions and refuse their advice, was to create and foster a spirit, not of manly, but of jealous independence, and to produce in a new form that vicious state of relationship between class and class, which is at this day the worst evil in our social life—the repulsion of the classes of society from each other at all points except one, so as to leave them touching at the single point of pecuniary interest. And thus the cementing principle of society is declared to be the spirit of selfishness—the only spirit which is essentially destructive. A fatal blunder!

When it is reckoned the duty of one class to give money, and the duty of another to suspect motives, the cordial sympathy of classes which really depend on another, cannot long continue. Not by mutual independence, but by mutual and trustful dependence, can men live together and society exist. As might have been expected, contributions fell off, and the more active and turbulent, unbalanced by a salutary check, became leaders in the Society.

An attempt was made by a numerous minority to introduce into the library works of skeptical and socialist principles. The secretary resisted the attempt. A general meeting of the members was dissolved without coming to a decision. In this emergency the following Address was made, with the intention of meeting that attempt, if possible, by a candid and pacific examination of the principles of the question.

An Address delivered to the Members of the Working Man's Institute, at the Town Hall, Brighton, on Thursday, April 18, 1850, *on the Question of the Introduction of Skeptical Publications into their Library.*

BROTHER MEN, MEMBERS OF THE WORKING MAN'S INSTITUTE.

Two years have passed since I addressed you in this place. On that occasion I was here by your invitation; on the present, you are here by mine. I have to explain the unprecedented step of summoning you to meet me here this evening. My account of it is this: I am personally compromised before the public by your proceedings. Unexpectedly on my part, you honoured me with a request that I would deliver the opening address to your society. It was at a period when events which had recently taken place upon the Continent, caused every large movement to be looked upon with suspicious eyes; yet I did not think it right to hesitate for one moment in complying with your request. Such influence as my name could command, I gladly gave you. I have not the vanity to say that that influence was great, or that my name had weight with many: but it did weigh with some; and support was given you by them in reliance upon my representations. To them, and to the public generally, I stand pledged for the character of your society. For good or evil, my name is inseparably linked with yours. Your success is my success, and your failure is my shame. This is my claim to be heard, or rather the ground on which rests my duty to address you; and I ask your calm attention, not promising that every word I say will be acceptable to all; but I think I may promise, that not a word shall drop from me, which on mature reflection you will be able justly to call illiberal.

It may require, too, to be explained why this address is a public one, instead of being confined to the members of the Institute. Great publicity has been given to your late meetings by your own hand-bills, and by the press. I cannot disguise from you the fact, that much pain has been felt in Brighton in consequence of those proceedings. I cannot hide from you that much attention has been directed towards you, and that our meeting of this evening is looked to with great anxiety. I cannot conceal from you, that sympathy has been much chilled, that the cause of the education of the working classes has received a shock, and that the question of the desirableness of free institutions has become a matter with many of serious doubt. Therefore, as the scandal was public, I felt that the vindication must be public too. You asked me to stand by you at the hopeful beginning of your institution—I could not desert you in the moment of danger, and the hour of your unpopularity. I am here once more to say publicly, that whatever errors there may have been in the working out of the details, I remain unaltered in the conviction that the broad principle on which your society commenced, was a true one. I am here to identify myself in public again with you—to say that your cause is my cause, and your failure my failure. I am here to profess my unabated trust in the sound-heartedness and right feeling of the great majority of the working men of the Brighton Institute.

One more thing remains to be accounted for. You will ask me why this meeting differs in form so evidently from your usual meetings. The chairman is not your president, not your vice-president, not even a member of your society. This is my reason. I am here to-night in a position quite peculiar; a position of peculiar delicacy, difficulty, and independence. I am not the organ or spokesman of any party. I do not mix myself with any of the personalities of the question. I have taken counsel of no one of either party; nor, indeed, have I asked any one's advice upon the matter. I am anxious that neither the president, nor any section of the Institute, should be pledged to my views. I asked no one to share the responsibility of summoning this meeting, or that of its result. Let all the blame, if blame there be, rest on me. On my single responsibility, all is done. To make this evident to the public, with the entire and friendly concurrence of your president, Mr. Ricardo, I asked one to preside over us to-night, whose firmness, impartiality, and uprightness, are so well known to his fellow townsmen, as to determine beforehand what the tone and character of this meeting are to be. This is not a lecture, but an address.

It is painful to be obliged to say any thing of self; yet, for several reasons, I feel compelled to say a few words respecting the spirit in which I desire to address you.

I do not pretend to dictate, nor shall I assume the tone of insulting condescension. I know that many whom I address to-night, have minds of a strength and hardness originally greater than mine, though my advantages of education may have been superior. I am not about to try the power of priestcraft, nor to cajole or flatter you into the reception of my views. Let the working men dismiss from their minds the idea, if it exists, of any assumption of a liberal tone for the purpose of winning them. If I speak sentiments free and liberal, it is not because they are adopted as opinions, but because they are bound up with every fibre of my being. I could as soon part with my nature and being, as cease to think and speak freely. Let them not fancy that such language is assumed, as fit for a platform before which *they* stand. There are those of your own number who will tell you that, in another place, from my own pulpit, not before workmen, but before their masters, before the rich and titled of this country, I have held and hold this same tone, and taught Christianity as the perfect Law of Liberty. They can tell you that it has cost me something, and that I have brought upon myself in consequence no small share of suspicion, misrepresentation, and personal dislike. I do not say this in bitterness; I hold it to be a duty to be liberal and generous, even to the illiberal and narrow-minded; and it seems to me a pitiful thing for any man to aspire to be true and to speak truth, and then to complain in astonishment, that truth has not crowns to give, but thorns; but I say it in order that you and I may understand each other. Let the men of this association rest assured that they shall hear no cant from me. I am not before them even to preach the Gospel, but to meet them on broad common ground, to speak to them as a man addressing his brother men.

Again, my purpose to-night is not denunciation. If any man has come expecting to hear Socialism and Infidelity denounced, he will be disappointed. My firm conviction is, that denunciation does no good. Anathemas, whether thundered from church courts, from pulpits, or from platforms, are foolish and impotent. It is the principle of that Book, the spirit of which I desire for my guide throughout life, that the wrath of man worketh not the righteousness of God.

Let me explain why I refuse to denounce Infidelity.

I refuse to do so to-night, because it would be ungenerous. You have heard of a place called "Coward's Castle." Coward's Castle is that pulpit or that platform from which a man, surrounded by his friends, in the absence of his opponents, secure of applause and safe from a reply, denounces those who differ from him. I mean to invite no discussion to-night; and just because there can be no reply, if there were no better reason than that, there shall be no denunciation.

Your chairman has already told you that there is to be no debate; and I will explain to you why I have resolved on this. All topics are the fit subjects of free inquiry; but all are not the fit subjects of public discussion. And this, not because of any weakness in them, or uncertainty respecting their truth; but because of the very delicacy of the matter in question. There are some things too delicate and too sacred to be handled rudely without injury to truth. Nothing is more certain than the duty of filial love; but if it were made a question for discussion in a school debating club, I fancy the arrival at truth would be somewhat questionable. Exactly in proportion as a boy was good, tender, and affectionate, would he feel it difficult, rhetorically or logically, to defend his feelings; he would be conscious of a stammering tongue, and a crimsoned cheek, and perhaps be overwhelmed with confusion. Nor would it require much talent or wit to make his position seem absurd—it would only require a copious flow of ribaldry. For you know the old proverb, that between the sublime and the ridiculous there is but a single step; and the more sacred a subject is, the more easy is it to give it an absurd aspect. It would be in the power of any bad boy to raise a laugh at the expense of one better and more manly than himself, by representing him as under the guidance of his mother's apron string. In the very same way it would be easy enough to reduce the position of a religious man to one exquisitely ludicrous ; loud, rude taunts of spiritual subjection, timidity, support by leading strings, pointed with blasphemy and unscrupulous effrontery, would not demand much superiority of talent, but would effectually cover all chance of arriving at the truth with a cloud of dust. Therefore do I refuse to permit discussion this evening respecting the love which a Christian man bears to his Redeemer, a love more delicate far than the love which was ever borne to sister, or the adoration with which he regards his God, a reverence more sacred than man ever bore to mother. Therefore do I reject the infinite absurdity of a trial of such truth as the existence of a God by a show of hands.

Again, there shall be no denunciation, because infidelity is the vaguest of all charges. None is more freely, or more wantonly, or more cruelly hurled by man against man. Infidelity is often only the unmeaning accusation brought by timid persons, half conscious of the instability of their own belief, and furious against every one whose words make them tremble at their own insecurity. It is sometimes the cry of narrowness against an old truth under a new and more spiritual form. Sometimes it is the charge caught up at second-hand, and repeated as a kind of religious hue and cry, in profoundest ignorance of the opinions that are so characterized. Nothing is more melancholy than to listen to the wild, indiscriminate charges of Skepticism, Mysticism, Pantheism, Rationalism, Atheism, which are made by some of the weakest of mankind, who scarcely know the difference between Mesmerism and Mysticism. I hold it a Christian duty, to abstain from this foolish and wicked system of labelling men with names; to stand aloof from every mob, religious or irreligious in name, which resembles that mob at Ephesus, who shouted for two long hours, the more part knowing not wherefore they were come together.

When the most spiritual minds of the sixteenth century protested against Rome, Protestantism was called infidelity. Eighteen centuries ago, the Christians were burned at the stake under the name of Atheists. The Athenians poisoned their noblest man as an Atheist. Only a few weeks ago, I saw one of the most precious works of one of the wisest of the Christian philosophers of England—Samuel Taylor Coleridge—denounced as the most pestilential work of our day, by one of those miserable publications, miscalled religious newspapers, whose unhallowed work it seems to be on earth to point out to its votaries whom they ought to suspect instead of whom they ought to love, and to sow the seeds of dissension, malice, hatred, and all uncharitableness. Nay, I cannot but remember that, in bygone years, One whose whole life was one continued prayer, the sum and substance of whose teaching was love to God and love to man, was crucified by the bigots of his day as a Sabbath-breaker, a Blasphemer, and a Revolutionist. Therefore I refuse to thunder out indiscriminate anathemas to-night. Real infidelity is a fearful thing, but I have learned to hold the mere *charge* of infidelity very cheap. And I earnestly would impress on all, the duty of being cautious in the use of these charges. Give a man the name of Atheist, hint that he is verging upon infidelity, and the man is doomed; doomed as surely as the wretched animal which is pursued by the hue and cry of bad boys, and which, driven from street to street, maddened by the ceaseless rattle of the tin appended to him, expires at last, gasping, furious, amidst the shrieks of old women, and the stones of terrified passengers, who are all the more savage in proportion to their terror. For cowardice is always cruel.

Again, I abstain from denunciation, because, not unfrequently, even that which professes to be infidelity, is disbelief, not of God, but of the character which men have given of God; opposition to the name of Christ, but not to the Spirit of Christ; hatred rather of the portrait by which his followers have represented him. I believe we should never forget, that if infidelity be rife in this country, we who profess to be servants of God, have much to answer for. Our bitterness and superstition, and rancour, have been the representations of the spirit of Christianity from which men have recoiled. Dare we brand infidelity with hard names, as if we were guiltless?

Ever the lesson of history has been this—the recoil from formalism is skepticism; the reaction from superstition is infidelity. In the days of the Pharisees, the natural and inevitable recoil was Sadduceeism. In the 15th and 16th centuries, when Christianity itself had become form and magic, the result was the polished infidelity of the Papal Court of the tenth Leo. When Puritanism had bound men's consciences by a strictness more intolerable than that of Popery itself, substituted a Pharisaism of words for a Pharisaism of ceremonies, regulated the simplicities of human life by a rigorous proscription of all free-hearted mirth, and even restricted the dishes on the table to a religious number,—the reaction was the light, skeptical licentiousness of the reign of Charles II. It is a fact worthy of deep pondering, to me a singularly startling one, that at the moment when we, the priests of England, were debating, as a matter of life and death, the precise amount of miracle said to be performed in a Christian sacrament, and excommunicating one another with reciprocated charges of heresy,—the working men of this country, who are not to be put off with transcendental hypotheses, and mysterious phraseology, on whom the burdens of this existence press as fearful realities, were actually debating in *their* societies, here beneath this very roof, a far more awful question, whether there be indeed a God or not. It might suggest to one who thinks, a question not altogether calming in these days, what connection there is between these two things.

There is a special reason for saying all this. Among the list of books proposed by one party amongst you, and rejected by the other, I find "Queen Mab," by Shelley. Now Shelley's works, if objectionable, are objectionable on a very different ground from that on which many similar works should be condemned. In one sense, Shelley was an infidel; in another sense, he was not an infidel. I could read you passages from

"Queen Mab," which every right-minded man, would indignantly condemn; and I could read you others breathing a spirit of benevolence, and aspiration, and trust, and purity, which are as sublime as poetically beautiful. Of the first class, I need scarcely say that I shall produce none; and of the second class, I will only quote one—

> "For when the power of imparting good
> Is equal to the will, the human soul
> Requires no other heaven."

I do not ask for a more spirited or a more just idea of heaven. Compare it with words infallible —"If we love one another, God dwelleth in us;" "It is more blessed to give than to receive." I would that the anticipated heaven of many who are called Christians, were half as much purged of the idea of arbitrary rewards, and happified selfishness.

I could adduce numbers of such passages. The poem is full of them, steeped in a flood of earnest desire to see this earth regenerated, and purified, and the spirit of man mingling with the Infinite Spirit of Good.

How comes it, then, that one whose works breathe so much of the spirit of Christianity, could blaspheme Christ? Alas! Christ had been miserably shown to Shelley. Poor, poor Shelley!

All that he knew of Christianity, was as a system of exclusion and bitterness, which was to drive him from his country; all that he knew of the God of the Bible, was the picture of a bloody tyrant, gloating in blood, and making his horrible decree the measure of right and wrong, instead of right and wrong the ground of his decree. I say God had been so represented to Shelley; and if it be replied, "Shelley might have read his Bible to find that this was false," I reply, that chapter and verse were quoted by those who were supposed to know their Bible, in corroboration of their theories, and Shelley could not have read those passages but with preconceptions of their meaning. I grieve that I cannot call Shelley a Christian. There are frantic ravings in this book which no Christian can justify; wild, vague music, as of an Æolian harp, inarticulate and unmeaning, breathed as a hymn to the Spirit of Nature, Intellectual Beauty, and so forth; maddest schemes and fastidious sensitivenesses respecting marriage, and man's granivorous nature; a fibre of insanity in his brain; yet I cannot help feeling that there was a spirit in poor Shelley's mind, which might have assimilated with the Spirit of his Redeemer,—nay which I will dare to say, was kindred with that Spirit, if only his Redeemer had been differently imaged to him.

Let who will denounce Shelley, I will not. I will not brand with Atheism the name of one whose life was one dream of enthusiastic however impracticable, philanthropy. I will not say that a man who, by his opposition to God, means opposition to a demon, to whom the name of God in his mind is appended, is an enemy of God. To such a man I only reply, you are blaspheming a devil. That is not the God I adore. You are not my enemy. Change the *name*, and I will bid that *character* defiance with you.

Once more, I do not denounce, because the state of Atheism is too miserable for me to curse it. There is an infidelity with which no good man should have any sympathy. There are infidels who are such, knowing what they oppose. There are men who, in no mistake, know the difference between good and evil, and distinctly knowing it, choose the evil and reject the good. But there is a state *called* infidelity, which deserves compassion rather than indignation—the dreadful state of one who craves light and cannot find it. I do think the way we treat that state, is most unpardonably cruel. It is an awful moment when the soul begins to find that the props on which it has blindly rested so long, are, many of them, rotten, and begins to suspect them all; when it begins to feel the nothingness of many of the traditionary opinions which have been received with implicit confidence, and in that horrible insecurity begins also to doubt whether there be any thing to believe at all. It is an awful hour — let him who has passed through it say how awful—when this life has lost its meaning, and seems shrivelled into a span; when the grave appears to be the end of all, human goodness nothing but a name, and the sky above this universe a dead expanse, black with the void from which God himself has disappeared. In that fearful loneliness of spirit, when those who should have been his friends and counsellors only frown upon his misgivings, and profanely bid him stifle doubts, which for aught he knows may arise from the fountain of truth itself, to extinguish, as a glare from hell, that which for aught he knows may be light from Heaven, and every thing seem wrapped in hideous uncertainty, I know but one way in which a man may come forth from his Agony scathless; it is by holding fast to those things which are certain still — the grand, simple landmarks of morality. In the darkest hour through which a human soul can pass, whatever else is doubtful, this at least is certain. If there be no God and no future state, yet, even then, it is better to be generous than selfish, better to be chaste than licentious, better to be true than false, better to be brave than to be a coward. Blessed beyond all earthly blessedness is the man who, in the tempestuous darkness of the soul, has dared to hold fast to these venerable landmarks. Thrice blessed is he, who, when all is drear and cheerless within and without, when his teachers terrify him, and his friends shrink from him, has obstinately clung to moral good. Thrice blessed, because *his* night shall pass into clear, bright day.

I appeal to the recollection of any man who has passed through that hour of agony, and stood upon the rock at last, the surges stilled below him, and the last cloud drifted from the sky above, with a faith, and hope, and trust, no longer traditional, but of his own, a trust which neither earth nor hell shall shake thenceforth for ever. But it is not in this way generally that men act who are tempted by doubt. Generally, the step from doubt is a reckless plunge into sensuality. Then comes the darkening of the moral being; and then from uncertainty and skepticism it may be that the path lies unobstructed, sheer down into Atheism. But if there be one on earth who deserves compassion, it is the sincere, earnest, and—may I say it without risk of being misunderstood?—honest doubter. Let who will denounce him, I will not. I would stand by his side, and say, Courage, my brother! You are darkening your own soul; you are contradicting the meaning of your own existence. But God is your Father, and an Infinite Spirit seeks to mingle itself with yours.

I pass to the immediate question which has brought us together this evening.

The history of recent events is briefly this. About a fortnight ago certain books were introduced, or attempted to be introduced into this Institution. They were objected to—I must say, rightly objected to, by a large majority of the members of the Institution. Out of a society of 800 or 900 members, only 138 could be found to publicly advocate their reception. Now, in order to treat this matter fairly, I believe that the best way will be to endeavour to consider, what are the principles on which their introduction is urged. Looking over these papers which have come before the public, I think I discern three grounds on which their proposal is defended; the Rights of Free Inquiry; the Rights of Liberty; and the Rights of Democracy. I am content to argue the question on those three grounds.

Let us first consider the Rights of Free Inquiry. It is said, and with some degree of truth, that the reason of man is the supreme judge of all things, and that God's existence cannot be demonstrated to reason. I am quite ready to admit that, provided that we can first agree respecting the word "Reason." Very often a dispute arises from a mistake concerning words. In English, the word "Reason" has two meanings, and I do not know that I can find any two words that are exactly adapted to express those two meanings, which are included in one and the same word. But we will express them in this way. There is a Soul and there is a Mind; the Soul or Heart is different from the Mind, and the Reason is different from the Understanding.* The understanding is that by which a man becomes a mere logician and a mere rhetorician; it is simply that by which he reasons from the impressions received through the senses. There is an understanding in the beaver, and there is an understanding in the bee, by which it builds its habitation. The fox has it as well, and there we call it cunning. They can and do reason; but they have not Reason. There you see the ambiguity, the two meanings of the

* It is scarcely needful to remark, that this use of the two words in a special and technical sense, to denote a most important distinction between two things essentially different, is borrowed from Mr. Coleridge.

word. It is by this Understanding that man knows what is profitable and what is unprofitable for him, by which he can shape his life with prudence. If you mean, in using the word Reason, to say that Understanding cannot find out God, I am ready to agree with you.

There is an expression imputed to one of the members of the Working Man's Institute, which has been since denied; but it matters little whether it was rightly or mistakenly denied by the committee; it is this—that "if a man undertakes to prove the being of a God, he undertakes to prove too much." I know not whether he said it or not. If he did not say it, I will say it for him. I cannot *prove* the being of a God; if by proof, I mean that addressed to the Understanding. If I said I could, I should be guilty of the vilest Rationalism. I cannot *prove* any one of the highest truths, except to the Heart, the Soul, the Reason. I cannot prove to any man that sweet is better than sour. I cannot prove that good is better than evil to any man, unless there is a correspondence in his own being to the eternal difference between them. I cannot prove to any man that there is a sun, unless he has an eye to see it. I cannot prove that he is in a waking state, if he is in an illusion that he is in a dream. For even the proof I give, the impression my hand makes on his, is not that disputable? May not that proof be part of his dream? Has he not before now dreamed that he was awake? The fact is, that there are truths of sense addressed to the Understanding; there are others, and they the highest, which are addressed to the Reason. I will undertake to convict a man of idiocy, if he cannot see the proof that three angles of a triangle are equal to two right angles. I will undertake to prove him fit for a lunatic asylum, if he refuses to receive the evidence that the earth goes round the sun. But if I place before a man an argument resting on miracles or on prophecy, or the proof from design, or any of the proofs addressed to the understanding, he may be neither an idiot nor insane, and yet unable to feel its force. An old French proverb says, that "grand thoughts come from the heart." God must be felt by the Heart, intuitively perceived by the Reason, before he can be demonstrated to the Understanding. If a man does not feel in every fibre of his heart a Divine Presence, I cannot prove that it is there, or anywhere else. For the evidence of the Senses can never be more certain than the convictions of the Soul or Reason.

There are men always talking of rights, and never of duties; I do not expect that they should believe in God, nor could I prove God to such.

But let a man once feel the law of duty in his soul—let him feel within him as with the articulate distinctness of a living Voice, the Absolute Imperative, "Thou shalt," and "Thou shalt not," —let him feel that the only hell is the hell of doing wrong, and if that man does not believe a God, all history is false. Brother men, the man who tries to discover a God outside of him instead of within, is doing just like him who endeavours to find out the place of the rainbow by hunting for it. The place of the rainbow depends upon your standing-point; and I say that the conviction of the being and character of a God, depends upon your moral standing-point. To believe in God, is simply the most difficult thing in the world. You must be pure before you can believe in purity; generous, before you can believe in unselfishness. In all moral truth, what you are, that is the condition of your belief. Only to him in whom infinite aspirations stir, can an Infinite One be proved.

Now once more we will try this on the principle of Free Inquiry. I find, on reading over the papers issued by the committee and their opponents, that one party objects to the refusal to admit these books, on the ground that it is an attempt to crush free inquiry. Well, let there be free inquiry; let there be no attempt to stop free inquiry. There is no censorship of the press. We desire none. I would not, for 100,000*l.* an hour, that there should be any restrictions placed on the publishing of books. I would far rather that there was much less of censorship of opinion. I know that millions of books, infidel and bad books, swarm out of the press; and yet I would not wish to see them stopped by force, except, of course, such as are shocking to public decency. Great as are the evils of unchecked license in publishing and reading, the evil of permitting any person or persons to restrict either authoritatively, would be immeasurably greater. It is a part of the liberty of the country, part of the freedom we enjoy, part of the very peace and purity we have, that all these things are permitted to be matters of free inquiry. It is part of our moral discipline. I would not have that exotic virtue which is kept from the chill blast, hidden from evil, without any permission to be exposed to temptation. That alone is virtue which has good placed before it and evil, and seeing the evil, chooses the good.*

But now, this loud cry about the bigotry of stopping free inquiry, let us consider it. What

* See the well-known passage in Milton's noble work, the "Areopagitica," which was unconsciously in the mind when these words were spoken.

do the objectors to these books say? Inquire if you will; only inquire at home. If you will read books of socialism or infidelity, read them at home, do not bring them into our institution. Do not compel the Working Man's Institute to indorse these books of yours with its approbation. Is this bigotry? Is this an attempt to stop free inquiry?

Now let us try the matter on the principle of Freedom. It seems to me that false notions respecting liberty are strangely common. People talk of liberty as if it meant the liberty of doing what a man *likes*. The only liberty that a man, worthy the name of a man, ought to ask for, is to have all restrictions, inward and outward, removed which prevent his doing what he *ought*. I call that man free, who is master of his lower appetites, who is able to rule himself. I call him free, who has his flesh in subjection to his spirit; who fears doing wrong, but who fears neither man nor devil besides. I think that man free, who has learnt the most blessed of all truths, that liberty consists in obedience to the power and to the will and to the law that his higher soul reverences and approves. He is not free because he does what he likes, for in his better moments his soul protests against the act, and rejects the authority of the passion which commanded him, as an usurping force, and tyranny. He feels that he is a slave to his own unhallowed passions. But he is free when he does what he ought, because there is no protest in his soul against that submission.

Some people seem to think that there is no liberty in obedience. I tell you there is no liberty *except* in loyal obedience—the obedience of the unconstrained affections. Did you never see a mother kept at home, a kind of prisoner, by her sick child, obeying its every wish and caprice, passing the night sleepless? Will you call the mother a slave? Or is this obedience the obedience of slavery? I call it obedience of the highest liberty, the liberty of love.

We hear in these days a great deal respecting Rights: the rights of private judgment, the rights of labour, the rights of property, and the rights of man. Rights are grand things, divine things in this world of God's; but the way in which we expound those rights, alas! seems to me to be the very incarnation of selfishness. I can see nothing very noble in a man who is for ever going about calling for his own rights. Alas! alas! for the man who feels nothing more grand in this wondrous, divine world than his own rights!

Let me tell you a story respecting rights.

Three thousand years ago, history tells us of two men, the one a poor man, the other a rich man. The name of the poor man was David, the name of the rich man was Nabal. David had been expelled from his country unjustly, and in that emergency there was nothing left for him but to secure his independence by becoming chieftain over a band of disaffected men, who lived in those rude times irregularly enough, but whose wild proceedings he contrived partially to restrain. There was a custom in that country which gave to every such chieftain a right to levy a kind of compulsory wages, tax, or black mail, upon those shepherds and farmers whose property he had respected and defended from others more unscrupulous. It had grown up by a kind of tacit understanding; not precisely defined, and liable therefore to considerable abuse and uncertainty. David had made such a claim on Nabal, and Nabal considered it unreasonable, refused to accede to it, and added, besides, words of taunt, those bitter, contemptuous words, which the arrogant vulgar can use, who fancy that wealth and birth have entitled them to scorn plebeian claims; words which make the blood boil in men's veins; whereupon David girded on his sword in fury, and nothing but an abject apology from Nabal's wife could have prevented an appeal to arms, or, as you call it in these days, an appeal to physical force.

Brother men, these were the Rights of Labour opposed to the Rights of Property. I cannot see any thing noble in that. I cannot see any thing manly in that ferocious struggle between rich and poor; the one striving to take as much, and the other to keep as much as he can. The cry of "My rights, your duties!" I think we might change to something nobler. If we could learn to say, "My duties, your rights," we should come to the same thing in the end; but the spirit would be different. That not very dignified feud between Nabal and David is only a picture of that which, hidden under fine names, men are calling now patriotism, public spirit, political martyrdom, protection, free trade—miserable enough in my mind.

All we are gaining by this cry of Rights, is the life of the wild beast and of the wild man of the desert, whose hand is against every man, and every man's hand against him. Nay, the very brutes, unless they had an instinct which respects Rights even more strongly than it claims them, could never form anything like a community. Did you never observe in a heronry or rookery, that the new-made nest is left in perfect confidence by the birds that build it? If the others had not learned to respect those private and sacred Rights, but began to assert each his right to the sticks which are woven together there, I fancy it would be some time before you could get a heronry or a rookery!

Two thousand years ago, there was One here on this earth who lived the grandest life that ever has been lived yet, a life that every thinking man, with deeper or shallower meaning, has agreed to call Divine. I read little respecting his Rights or of his claims of Rights; but I have read a great deal respecting his Duties. Every act He did he called a Duty. I read very little in that life respecting his Rights; but I hear a vast deal respecting his Wrongs—wrongs infinite—wrongs borne with a majestic, Godlike silence. His reward? His reward was the reward that God gives to all his true and noble ones—to be cast out in his day and generation, and a life-conferring death at last. Those were HIS Rights!

This, then, is the way in which we desire to expound Rights: my Rights are, in truth, my Duties; my Rights are limited by another man's Rights. For example, I have a perfect right to build a wall on my own estate. The language of the law is, that to whomsoever the soil belongs, is his all up to the skies. But within three yards of my wall is my neighbour's window. What becomes of the Right that I was talking of? My Right is limited; it is my duty, because limited by his Right.

You have a right to read your books and to inquire and to examine for yourselves; but I put it to you, brother men, have you a right to force into an institution shared by others, books which are to them disgusting? Is that liberty?

There is one other principle on which the present arrangement of your affairs is defended. It is the rights of Democracy. I will now define Democracy. I know not whether the definition will be taken; but I will give it in the fair, and generous, and candid sense. I believe that in everything held with earnestness by large bodies of men, there is a certain amount of truth. Whether I hold democratic views or not, is not the question. I merely endeavour to expound the fair meaning of them. Now, Democracy, if it means anything, means government by the people. It has for its very watchword, Equality of all men. Now let us not endeavour to make it ridiculous. I suppose that a sensible democrat does not mean that all individual men are equal in intelligence and worth. He does not mean that the Bushman or the Australian is equal to the Englishman. But he means this—that the original stuff of which all men are made, is equal; that there is no reason why the Hottentot and the Australian may not be cultivated, so that in the lapse of centuries they may be equal to Englishmen. I suppose the democrat would say, there is no reason why the son of a cobbler should not by education become fit to be the prime minister of the land, or take his place on the bench of judges. And I suppose that all free institutions mean this. I suppose they are meant to assert—Let the people be educated; let there be a fair field and no favour; let every man have a fair chance, and then the happiest condition of a nation would be, that when every man had been educated morally and intellectually to his very highest capacity, there should then be selected out of men so trained a Government of the Wisest and the Best.

This is the principle of Democracy. I suppose no man will quarrel with this definition. It appears to me that you have departed from that principle. The principle of Democracy is this—that there is no essential difference between man and man; no reason why one class should be selected for privileges as, in its nature, necessarily superior to another class. I find in your book of rules, a rule which entirely contradicts that; and it seems to me that it is a suicidal rule. It is this. You have a rule which prevents any one of your honorary, that is richer members, from having a vote or acting in committee. That is to say, you will neither have a Democracy nor an Aristocracy, but an Oligarchy. Not an open field for worth, nor a government by the best and wisest; but a government by a specified class. You will not permit the intelligence of others to guide or assist you. You cut yourselves off from all more highly educated minds. You not only say that the working man, intellectually and originally, is on a level with others, but that he is absolutely superior. You deny Equality. You will not permit a free, fair chance for a government of the wisest and best. You say the most ignorant must be the best and wisest. Is that Democracy? Brother men, I hesitate not to say, that unless that rule be rescinded, and the whole thing be put on a different footing, this institution is lost. I know that this was done with the concurrence of your late lamented treasurer. It was not a rule which I felt could ever succeed or prosper; but, however, so long as his influence was with you, which you respected and revered, the injury was not felt, because he supplied the place of that intelligence from which you have cut yourselves off. But let that rule remain, live in the spirit of jealousy and suspicion, believe that the upper classes mean you ill, that in the great town of

Brighton no man of any rank or wealth above your own can assist you with advice but he must do so from interested motives, and I can not see how this institution is to last at all.

I now wish to put before you two or three reasons why it seems to me that, on grounds of fairness, these books ought to be rejected. The first reason is, that they are contrary to the very objects of your institution. I find in the address put forth by the committee to the members, these words: "We are only carrying out the objects of our institution and the wishes of its members, by affording mental amusement for all tastes of our supporters." I will not severely criticize that sentence, though it lies open to much criticism. I have a much more important work before me than the criticism of sentences. I am willing to admit that it is loosely expressed, and I do not wish to take advantage of an incorrect expression. There are members of this institution little above twelve or thirteen years of age; and if I wanted to turn it into ridicule, I might ask the committee whether they meant to say, in stating that principle, that they consider themselves bound to furnish books level to the capacity of children of thirteen years of age? There are persons among you, I fear it must be said, of licentious feelings; I am sure the members of the committee will not say they are bound to furnish mental amusement fitted to the taste of such persons. Yet if they mean any thing, they must mean this,—that if there be in the society a large body of working men who hold certain views and opinions, it is their bounden duty to provide intellectual food suited to each of such classes. For example: take the books objected to, and if there be a man who has a taste for socialism, it is then their duty to provide such books as Robert Owen's works; or, if there be a taste for infidelity, it is their bounden duty to furnish the works of Tom Paine; or, if a man descends in taste to a lower depth still, if he can revel in such works as the "Mysteries of London," it is the bounden duty of the committee to furnish him with books of that character. Admit that principle, and your society is shattered into fragments.

Let there be a change of expression. The true way of stating the principle, is this; not that it is their bounden duty to furnish mental food for all tastes, but that it is their duty to furnish books adapted for the tastes of all their supporters. There is an immense difference. If you lay down this principle, that they are bound to furnish books adapted to all tastes of supporters, then every taste must be represented. But if you say they are to furnish books for the tastes of all supporters, then they are bound to furnish those which shall meet the wishes of all, and be disagreeable to none, such as shall be suited to those tastes which are common to all. Let me give you a parallel case. In the higher classes of society, men of different ranks and attainments, and very various tastes, unite to form a society similar to yours. The clergyman, the medical man, and the lawyer, ladies and antiquaries, all join and form a lending library, book society, or whatsoever it may be called. Now it is plainly the duty of their committee to provide works which they may all read in common. There are certain tastes and principles in which they all agree. There is a large variety of books which meet all their tastes. This is the very principle of their union in a society. It is for this they have met and clubbed their money together. They perceive that they have certain tastes in common, and they combine, in order that they may be able to read more books than they could by buying them singly and separately. This is the principle.

Now suppose, instead of that, the committee were to resolve that there must be a shelf of divinity and a shelf of chemistry, for clergymen and medical men, and another shelf of black-letter books for antiquarians, and you will at once observe that the whole meaning of a society such as this is lost. The medical man and the clergyman join the general society to read books of general and not of special interest. If the clergyman wishes for his book of theology, and the medical man his medical authority, the one must form a clerical library, and the other must form his medical society. But in that case he must be content with limited numbers and limited means, exactly in proportion as the object of association becomes limited and definite. Precisely so with this Society. I do not say that the members of this Institute have not a perfect right to form unions amongst themselves; but once give utterance to this principle,—that it is the duty of the committee to furnish food for all tastes, then you will have, not a society but societies, not an institution, but a knot of clubs.

I call your attention to another point. In this paper, your committee hold it to be their duty to afford mental amusement for all tastes. Again I say, I will not rigorously press the exact meaning of words. It is a duty always to endeavour to ascertain what men mean, instead of ungenerously binding them by their words, which are often inexact. And, indeed, on looking at the titles of these books "of amusement," I find that some are any thing but amusing, but are books which require great exercise of intellectual faculties. But still some remark must be made on this idea of works of *amusement.* It is the duty of the committee, in *part,* to furnish books of amusement. I said so in my opening address. I was greatly sneered at for saying so. Many well-meaning and religious persons said I had forgotten my place as a clergyman in speaking of works of fiction as fit for labouring men. They were shocked and startled that I dared to reckon it a matter of rejoicing that there is a moral tone in that well-known publication which is dedicated to wit and humour, or that I even named it. They were scandalized that I could find any thing of moral significance in the works of Dickens. I stand to what I said. I do not like to characterize that kind of language severely; otherwise I should call it cant. It exhibits a marvellous ignorance of the realities and the manifoldness of human life. I am prepared to say that works of fiction and amusement must and will be read, and that they ought to be read. There is a deal of religion in an earnest, hearty laugh that comes ringing from the heart. That man is a bad man who has not within him the power of a hearty laugh. Therefore it cannot be denied that it is *part* of the duty of the committee to furnish works of amusement; but I cannot but acknowledge that it is a matter of surprise and regret, that, even by an oversight, the committee should have represented it as their duty *chiefly* to furnish works of mere mental amusement. Your Rule declares that " The objects of this Institution are to provide means for the moral and intellectual *improvement* of its members." What has become of that high moral tone which characterized your first addresses to the public? Where are the men from whom I have heard, in the room below, language which did my heart good, and made me feel proud of my country, which made me compare it triumphantly with the language that men of the working classes were holding on the other side of the water? Men of the Brighton Working Man's Institute! how comes it that the language of your publications now is so immeasurably inferior in moral tone?

Once more, you owe it to the cause in which your society is enlisted, to reject peremptorily these infidel publications.

Every man, if he is not deterred by feeling for his own character, is deterred by feeling for his cause. There are many things that a soldier will do in his plain clothes which he scorns to do in his uniform. You have a cause, and I must acknowledge that the cause has received a severe blow by the proceedings of your last public meeting. I must admit, as I said before, that free institutions are looked upon now with eyes of jealousy and suspicion by many who lately felt towards them very favourably. I have heard again and again this taunt,—"These are your friends, the working men; this comes of your philanthropy." And others, in a less bitter spirit, have said, "I fear you will be disappointed in your hopes of these working men." My friends, the working men! Would to God they were my friends. Would to God I were more their friend. I look back once more two thousand years, and dare not forget Who it was that was born into this world the Son of a poor woman, and probably laboured for thirty years in a carpenter's shop, a *Working Man!*

In reply to that sarcasm, I observe, it is to be remembered that the first use a man makes of every power and talent given to him, is a bad use. The first time a man ever uses a flail, it is to the injury of his own head and of those who stand around him. The first time a child has a sharp-edged tool in his hand, he cuts his finger. But this is no reason why he should not be ever taught to use a knife. The first use a man makes of his affections, is to sensualize his spirit.

Yet he cannot be ennobled, except through those very affections. The first time a kingdom is put in possession of liberty, the result is anarchy. The first time a man is put in possession of intellectual knowledge, he is conscious of the approaches of skeptical feeling. But that is no proof that liberty is bad, or that instruction should not be given. There is a moment in the ripening of the fruit when it is more austere and acid than in any other. It is not the moment of greenness, the moment when it is becoming red, the transition state, when it is passing from sourness into sweetness. It is a law of our humanity, that man must know both good and evil; he must know good *through* evil. There never was a principle but what triumphed through much evil; no man ever progressed to greatness and goodness but through great mistakes.

There have been great mistakes made in this society, and there are many difficulties; but you will weather the difficulties yet. The mistakes will become your experience. Nay, I believe that the discipline of character which many of you will have gained by this struggle with an evil principle, and the practical insight which it has given you into the true bearing of many social questions, in which I personally know that wild and captivating theories have been modified in your minds by this recent experience, will be invaluable. If only this had been gained, I believe the institution would not have been established in vain. But if men say that all these difficulties tell against inquiry and education, I can only say that it proves we want more education. If I wanted a proof of that, I should find it in this,—that the working men of Brighton have not yet got beyond Tom Paine.

This, then, brother men, is the reply to the taunts that have been made use of. But still I am bound to acknowledge this,—and I do it with shame and sorrow,—that there has been a handle put, by some of yourselves, into the hand of the bigot and the timid man. What then, is all that the tyrants of the past have said, true; and all that the philanthropists have said, false? Were all their gloomy predictions sagaciously prophetic? What have the tyrant, the bigot, and the timid said? That it is impossible to give power to the people without making them revolutionary, or to give them instruction without making them infidel. You owe it to yourselves and to your cause to cast the imputation from you. And if Infidelity presumes to lay her hand upon the ark of your magnificent and awful cause, the cause of the people's liberty, and men say that it is part and parcel of the system, give that slander to the winds, and prove, men of Brighton, by the rejection of these books, and by the reorganization of your society, that the cause of instruction and the cause of freedom are not the cause of infidelity.

TWO LECTURES

ON

THE INFLUENCE OF POETRY

ON THE

WORKING CLASSES.

Two Lectures on the Influence of Poetry on the Working Classes, delivered before the Members of the Mechanics' Institution, February, 1852.

LECTURE I.*

THE selection of the subject of this evening's Lecture, "The Influence of Poetry on the Working Classes," requires some explanation. What has Poetry to do with the Working Classes? What has it, in fact, to do with this age at all? Does it not belong to the ages past, so that the mere mention of it now is an anachronism—something out of date? Now, there is a large class of persons, to whom all that belongs to our political and social existence seems of such ab-

* As some of the topics contained in the following Lectures might seem out of place, as addressed to the members of a Mechanics' Institution, it may be well to state that they were delivered before a mixed audience. They are printed, with some additions, from the corrected notes of a short-hand reporter.

sorbing interest, that they look with impatience on any thing which does not bear directly on it. A great political authority of the present day has counselled the young men of this country, and especially of the Working Classes, not to waste their time on literature, but to read the newspapers, which, he says, will give them all the education that is essential. Persons of this class seem to fancy that the all-in-all of man is "to get on;" according to them, to elevate men means, chiefly, to improve their circumstances; and, no doubt, they would look with infinite contempt on any effort such as this, to interest men on subjects which, most assuredly, will not give them cheaper food or higher wages. "Lecture them," they will say, "on the principles of political economy, in order to stem, if possible, the torrent of those dangerous opinions that threatens the whole fabric of society. Give them, if you will, lectures on science, on chemistry, on mechanics, on any subject which bears on real and actual life; but, really, in this work-day age, rhyming is out of place and out of date. We have no time for Poetry and prettiness." If, indeed, to have enough to eat and enough to drink were the whole of man—if the highest life consisted in what our American brethren call "going a-head"—if the highest ambition for

Working Men were the triumph of some political faction, then, assuredly, the discussion of our present subject would be waste of breath and time.

But it appears to me, that in this age of Mechanics and Political Economy, when every heart seems "dry as summer dust," what we want is, not so much, not half so much—light for the intellect, as dew upon the heart; time and leisure to cultivate the spirit that is within us. The author of "Philip Van Artevelde," in his last published volume, "The Eve of the Conquest," has well described this our state of high physical civilization and refinement, in which knowledge is mistaken for wisdom, and all that belongs to man's physical comfort and temporal happiness is sedulously cared for, while much that belongs to our finer and purer being is neglected — an age of grim earnestness — not the noble earnestness of stern Puritanism for high principles, but one which is terrible only when the purse is touched.

"Oh, England! 'Merry England,' styled of yore!
Where is thy mirth? Thy jocund laughter where?
The sweat of labour on the brow of care
Makes a mute answer: driven from every door.
The May-pole cheers the village-green no more,
Nor harvest-home, nor Christmas mummers rare,

The tired mechanic at his lecture sighs,
And of the learned, which, with all his lore,
Has leisure to be wise ?"

Whatever objection may deservedly belong to this Lecture, I hope that no "tired mechanic" will sigh over its tediousness or solemnity. I believe that recreation is a holy necessity of man's nature; and it seems to me by no means unworthy of a sacred calling to bestow an hour on the attempt to impart not uninstructive recreation to Working Men.

There are some other objections, however, connected with the subject, which must be noticed. Poetry may be a fitting study for men of leisure, but it seems out of the question for Working Men;—a luxury for the rich, but to attempt to interest the poor in it, is as much out of place as to introduce them into a cabinet of curiosities, or a gallery of pictures. I believe such a feeling has arisen partly from this cause—that the Poetry of the last age was eminently artificial, unnatural, and aristocratic; it reflected the outer life of modern society and its manners, which are conventional, uniform, polished, and therefore unnatural, and not of general human interest. I will read to you a description of that which one of the poets of that age thought to be the legitimate call and mission of the poet. Thus writes Pope:—

"Poetry and criticism are by no means the universal concern of the world, but only the affair of idle men who write in their closets, and of idle men who read there . . . .

"All the advantages I can think of, accruing from a genius for Poetry, are the agreeable power of self-amusement, when a man is idle or alone; the privilege of being admitted into the best company, and the freedom of saying as many careless things as other people without being so severely remarked on."

You will scarcely wonder that when a poet could thus write of his art, working men and real men, who have no time for prettinesses, and have not the privilege of being "admitted into the best company," should be indifferent to Poetry, and that it should have come to be reckoned among the luxuries of the wealthy and idle; nor will you be surprised that one who thought so meanly of his high work and duty, should never, with all his splendid talents, have attained to any thing in Poetry beyond the second rank, that in which thought and memory predominate over imagination, and in which the heart is second to the head; for much of Pope's Poetry is nothing more than ethical thoughts tersely and beautifully expressed in rhyme.

There is another reason, however, for this misconception. The Poetry of the present age is, to a great extent, touched, tainted if you will, with mysticism. Let us trace the history of this.

A vigorous protest was made at last against the formalism of the Poetry of the last century. The reaction began with Wordsworth, Scott, and Byron, and the age of conventional Poetry was succeeded by the Poetry of sentiment and passion. But, by degrees, this wave also spent itself; and another came. Wordsworth was the poet of the few; the border minstrelsy of Scott exhausted itself even during his own life; and when that long, passionate wail of Byronism had died away,—a phase of tempestuous feeling through which every man, I suppose, passes in one portion or other of his existence—men began to feel that this life of ours was meant for something higher than for a man to sit down to rave and curse his destiny; that it is at least manlier, if it be bad, to make the best of it, and do what may be done. Next came, therefore, an age whose motto was "Work." But now, by degrees, we are beginning to feel that even work is not all our being needs; and, therefore, has been born what I have called the Poetry of Mysticism. For just as the reaction from the age of Formalism was the Poetry of Passion, so the reaction from the age of Science, is, and I suppose ever will be, the Poetry of Mysticism. For men who have felt a want which work cannot altogether satisfy, and have become conscious that the clear formulas and accurate technicalities of science have not expressed, nor ever can, the truths of the Soul, find a refuge in that vagueness and undefined sense of mystery which broods over the shapeless borders of the illimitable. And thus the very mystic obscurity of thought and expression which belongs to Browning, Tennyson, and even Wordsworth, is a necessary phase in the history of Poetry, and is but a protest and witness for the infinite in the soul of man.

For these two reasons, that the Poetry of the past age was conventional and that of the present mystical, it was very natural that Poetry should have come to be reckoned merely an amusement, suited to men of leisure. But it was not always so: Poetry began, not in the most highly civilized, but in the half-civilized stages of society. The Drama, for example, was first acted in wagons drawn through the Grecian villages, and performed by men who only half-concealed their personality by the rude expedient of smearing the face with the lees of wine. And, before that, the poems of Homer had been recited with enthusiasm in the villages and cities of Ionia, by the people. The poems of Burns, himself a peasant, are the darling favourites of the Scottish peasant, and lie with his Bible, on the same shelf.

And where did our own English Poetry begin, but in those popular ballads of which you have a notable example in the epic ballad of "Chevy Chase?" Poetry is essentially of the people, and for the people.

However, it will be granted, perhaps, that the love of Poetry is compatible with an incomplete education; but hardly with a want of leisure, or with hard work. To this I reply, first, by a matter of fact: the works of Poetry in this Institution, since the loss of its first large library, are few; but those few are largely read. Upon the librarian, constant demands are made for the works of Shakspeare and Sir Walter Scott.

I reply, secondly: I know something myself of hard work; I know what it is to have had to toil when the brain was throbbing, the mind incapable of originating a thought, and the body worn and sore with exhaustion; and I know what it is in such an hour, instead of having recourse to those gross stimulants to which all worn men, both of the higher and lower classes, are tempted, to take down my Sophocles or my Plato (for Plato was a poet), my Goethe, or my Dante, Shakspeare, Shelley, Wordsworth, or Tennyson; and I know what it is to feel the jar of nerve gradually cease, and the darkness in which all life had robed itself to the imagination become light, discord pass into harmony, and physical exhaustion rise by degrees into a consciousness of power. I cannot, and I will not, believe that this is a luxury, or rather a blessed privilege, reserved for me, or my class, or caste, alone. If I know from personal experience—and I do know—that feelings such as these, call them romantic if you will, can keep a man all his youth through, before a higher Faith has been called into being, from every species of vicious and low indulgence, in every shape and every form,—if I believe that there are thousands,

> "Whose hearts the holy forms
> Of young imagination have kept pure,"

I am compelled also to believe that, as that which is human belongs to all humanity, so there is power in this pursuit to enable the man of labour to rise sometimes out of his dull, dry, hard toil, and dreary routine of daily life, into forgetfulness of his state, to breathe a higher and serener, and purer atmosphere. I *will* believe that for him, too, there is an

> "Appeal to that imaginative power,
> Which can commute a sentence of sore pain
> For one of softer sadness."

Some years ago, an Irishman, scarcely above a peasant in rank, was employed on the Ordnance

Survey, under an officer of Engineers, in Suffolk, where I then was. I remember the description he gave me of the state of the Irish peasantry, and the scenes of wretchedness I had not then witnessed: "Their cabins, your honour," said he, "are in such a state sometimes, that the poor craturs could count the stars as they lay on their beds."

I am not prepared to dispute that it might have been better for the Irish peasant if, instead of lying on his bed counting the stars and cursing the Saxon, he had got up and mended his roof; nor will I enter into the question whether seven hundred years of English misrule have darkened all hope in the nation's breast, and left them neither heart nor spirit to mend and patch a hopeless lot; but I think you will agree with me, that a hard-working man, to whose imagination the thought which spontaneously presented itself on the sight of a roofless hut, was, not that of dripping rain or driving winds, but of poor creatures lying on their beds to count the stars, who could get away from discomfort to expatiate in the skies, was, to some extent, through his imagination and his poetry, independent of external circumstances.

By the title of this Lecture I am bound to define, in the first place, what is meant by

"Poetry;" and, in the second, to endeavour to sustain the assertion "that it has a powerful influence on the Working Classes."

The former of these is the subject of this first Lecture. Our first definition of Poetry is—the natural language of excited feeling. When a man is under the influence of some strong emotion, his language, words, demeanour, become more elevated; he is twice the man he was. And not only his words, and posture, and looks, but the whole character and complexion of his thoughts are changed. They belong to a higher order of imagination, and are more full of symbolism, and imagery; the reason of which is—that all the passions deal not with the limitations of time and space, but belong to a world which is infinite. The strong passions, whether good or bad, never calculate. Anger, for example, does not ask for satisfaction in gold and silver; it feels and resents a wrong that is infinite; Love demands the eternal blessedness of the thing loved—it feels, and delights to feel that it is itself infinite, and can never end; Revenge is not satisfied with temporary pain, but imprecates the perdition of the offender.

And so, these passions of ours, uncalculating, and outlaws of time and space, disdaining the bounds of the universe,

"Glancing from heaven to earth, from earth to heaven,"

never argue, but reach at a single bound the eternal truth, discover unexpected analogies hidden before through all the universe, and subordinate each special case to some great and universal law.

Hence, the language of strong emotion is always figurative, symbolical, and rich in metaphors. For the metaphors of Poetry are not mere ornaments stuck on, and capable of being taken off without detriment to the essence of the thought. They are not what the clothes are to the body, but what the body is to the life—born with it; the form in which the life has been clothed, without which the life would have been impossible; just as Minerva is fabled by the ancients to have risen in full panoply out of the brain of Jupiter.

Poetry, I have said, is the *natural* language of excited feeling. It is not something invented or artificial, but that in which excited feeling naturally clothes itself. Now take an example. When the Pragmatic Sanction was violated on all sides in Europe, when Silesia had been wrested away by the young King of Prussia, and, with the assistance and sanction of the French, the Elector of Bavaria was aiming at the Crown of the Empire, the Empress Maria Theresa threw herself on her Hungarian subjects. We are told that when, robed in black, she appeared in the Diet, with her child in her arms, and asked their assistance, the Hungarian nobles rose, and with one voice, exclaimed, "Let us die for our King, Maria Theresa!" Observe the poetry of the expression, "our *King* Maria Theresa." No calculation in that moment; no mercenary sordidness, balancing the question whether a nation could afford to defend weakness and honour at the expense of a costly war, or not. They had risen in one moment of strong emotion to the highest truth of human existence, the Law of Sacrifice; they had penetrated into that region in which kingly qualities had blended together the two sexes, and broken down the whole barrier of distinction between man and woman; that region in which tenderness and loyalty are not two, but one: "Let us die for our KING, Maria Theresa!"

You will perceive from this that there is an element of poetry in us all. Whatever wakes up intense sensibilities, puts you for a moment into a poetic state; if not the creative state, that in which we can *make* poetry, at least the receptive state in which we *feel* poetry. Therefore, let no man think that, because he cannot appreciate the verse of Milton or Wordsworth, there is no poetry in his soul; let him be assured that there is something within him which may any day awake, break through the crust of his selfishness, and redeem him from a low, mercenary, or sensual existence.

Any man who has for a single moment felt those emotions which are uncalculating, who has ever risked his life for the safety of another, or met some great emergency with unwavering courage, or felt his whole being shaken with mighty and unutterable indignation against some base cruelty or cowardly scoundrelism, knows what I mean when I say that there is something in him which is infinite, and which can transport him in a moment into the same atmosphere which the poet breathes.

"High instincts," Wordsworth calls them,

> "Before which our mortal nature
> Did tremble, like a guilty thing surprised:
> . . . . . . those first affections,
> Those shadowy recollections
> Which, be they what they may,
> Are yet the Fountain-light of all our day,
> Are yet the master-light of all our seeing:
> Uphold us, cherish, and have power to make
> Our noisy years seem moments in the being
> Of the Eternal Silence. Truths that wake,
> To perish never."

Shakspeare, who knew all that man can feel,

and the times when he feels it, is here, as usual, true to nature. You must have observed that he never puts language highly imaginative, what we call Poetry, into the lips of any except exalted characters, who may be supposed to live in Poetry, or persons who, for the time, are under some exciting influence. If you will compare the manner and expression of Timon of Athens, through the earlier acts, with his language in the latter part of the Play, you will see how he becomes another man under the influence of a powerful passion. At first, you have the high-born, high-bred gentleman, magnificent in his liberality, and princely in his tastes, bestowing a fortune on a dependent whose poverty is the sole bar to a happy marriage, giving away the bay courser to his guest because he admired it; the munificent patron of the arts, using the conventional language and the flat, dead politeness of polished society, with no strong feeling of life, because nothing has broken the smoothness of its current. But the shock comes. In temporary reverses he begins to feel the hollowness of friendship, suspects that men and women are not what they seem; and then, with that passionate scorn which henceforth marks his character, the real poetry of Timon's existence begins. And this is made the more remarkable by the relief in which his character stands out from the contrast between two misanthropes in the same Play. One is the generous Timon, who has despaired of men because he has not found them what he expected them to be; the other, the self-enclosed Apemantus, who believes in the meanness of all human natures because he is mean himself. Even when the two reciprocate abuse, the distinction is preserved. Apemantus is merely scurrilous—"beast" and "toad" are the epithets of his vocabulary. One pregnant word, alive with meaning, falls from Timon's lips—"Slave." And then, disappointed in his best and highest affections, the whole universe appears to his disordered imagination overspread with the guilt of his wrongs: earth and skies and sea are robbers; yet his scorn is lofty still; even gold, the general seducer, he does not curse with the low invective of the conventicle.

Listen to the impassioned scorner:—

"Thou ever young, fresh, lov'd, and delicate wooer,
Whose blush doth thaw the consecrated snow
That lies on Dian's lap! Thou visible god,
That solder'st close impossibilities,
And mak'st them kiss! That speak'st with every tongue
To every purpose! O, thou touch of hearts!"

It is poetry throughout—passion rendered imaginative; scorn, as contrasted with mere spite.

In saying, however, that Poetry is the language

of excited feeling, by excitement is not to be understood mere violence or vehemence; but intensity. It is with accurate knowledgè of human nature that Philip Van Arteveldè says to Sir Fleuréant, who is imploring forgiveness with vehement self-reproach: "Thou art a weak, inconstant, violent man." Weakness and violence often go together. Passion may be violent; as in the case of Othello, Lear, and Northumberland; it does not follow that it must; vehemence is simply dependent on physical organization, a mere matter of brain and nerve. Indeed, the most intense feeling is generally the most subdued and calm; for it is necessarily condensed by repression. A notable example you have in Wordsworth, the calmest of poets; so much so, that I have heard him characterized as a Quaker among poets. And yet he is the author of the sublimest ode in the English language, the Intimations of immortality from the recollections of childhood. And for his *intensity*, I only appeal to those who have understood his poetry, felt, and loved it.

Yet even in this apparent exception we have a corroboration of the rule. Intense as Wordsworth is, there is in him something wanting for the very highest poetry. He is too calm. There is a want of passion; and hence an entire absence of epic as well as dramatic power; he reflects when he ought to describe, and describes feeling when he ought to exhibit its manifestation. He sings of our nature as some philosophic spirit might sing of it in passionless realms of contemplation, far away from the discords of actual existence, of a humanity purged and purified, separate from the fierce feelings and wild gusts of passion which agitate real human life. And therefore Wordsworth never can be popular in the true sense of the word. His works will be bought and bound richly, and a few of his poems will be familiar words; but still he will remain the poet of the few; acknowledged by the many, only because he is reverenced by the few; those discerning few whose verdict slowly, but surely, leads the world at last.

I have said that Poetry is the natural language of intense feeling. It is in perfect accordance with this that the great master of all criticism, Aristotle, divides Poetry into two orders. He says a poet must be one of two things—a "frenzied man," or an "accomplished man;" in which single sentence are contained whole volumes. There are two kinds of poets; the one inspired, and the other skilful; the one borne away by his own feelings, of which he is scarcely master; the other able rather to conceive feelings and simulate their expression, than possessed by, or possessing them.

Hence it is almost proverbial that the poetic temperament, except in a few cases of felicitously organized constitution, and rare equilibrium of powers, is one of singular irritability of brain and nerve.

Even the placid Wordsworth says—

> "We poets in our youth begin with gladness;
> But thereof come in the end despondency and madness."

And by this, too, we can understand, and compassionate, I do not say excuse, the force of that temptation of stimulants to which so many gifted natures have fallen a sacrifice. Poetry is the language of excited feeling; properly of pure excitement. But stimulants, like wine, opium, and worse, can produce, or rather simulate, that state of rapturous and ecstatic feeling in which the seer should live; in which emotions succeed each other swiftly, and imagination works with preternatural power. Hence their seductive power.

Our higher feelings move our animal nature; and our animal nature, irritated, can call back a semblance of those emotions; but the whole difference between nobleness and baseness lies in the question whether feeling begins from below or above. The degradation of genius, like the sensualizing of passion, takes place when men hope to reproduce, through stimulus of the lower nature, those glorious sensations which it once experienced when vivified from above. Imagination ennobles appetites which in themselves are low, and spiritualizes acts which are else only animal. But the pleasures which *begin* in the senses only sensualize.

Burns and Coleridge are the awful beacons to all who feel intensely, and are tempted to rekindle the vestal flames of genius, when they burn low, with earthly fire.

I give another definition of Poetry. I think I have seen it defined—I am not sure whether I have confounded my own thoughts with what I have a dim recollection of having somewhere read—as "the indirect expression of feelings that cannot be expressed directly." We all have feelings which we cannot express. There is a world into which the poet introduces us, of which the senses are not the organs; there is a beauty which the eye has never seen, and a music which the ear has never heard. There are truths, eternally, essentially, and necessarily true, which we have never yet seen embodied. And there is, besides, from our human sympathies, a strong necessity for giving utterance to these cravings in us. For language has been given, not merely to make known our own selfish wants, but to impart ourselves to our fellow men. Now, if these intense feelings could be expressed directly, so that when you expressed them, you felt yourself understood as adequately as when you say "I thirst," or "I am hungry," then there would be no Poetry at all; but, because this is impossible, the soul clothes her intuitions, her aspirations, and forebodings, in those indirect images which she borrows from the material world.

For this reason the earliest language of all nations is Poetry. Language has been truly called fossil Poetry; and just as we apply to domestic use slabs of marble, unconscious almost that they contain the petrifactions of innumerable former lives, so in our every-day language we use the living Poetry of the past, unconscious that our simplest expressions are the fossil forms of feeling which once was vague, and laboured to express itself in the indirect analogies of materialism. Only think from whence came such words as "attention," "understanding," "imagination."

As language becomes more forcible and adequate, and our feelings are conveyed, or supposed to be conveyed, entirely, Poetry in words becomes more rare. It is then only the deeper and rarer feelings, as yet unexpressed, which occupy the poet. Science destroys Poetry; until the heart bursts into mysticism, and out of science brings Poetry again; asserting a wonder and a vague mystery of life and feeling, beneath and beyond all science, and proclaiming the wonderfulness and mystery of that which we seem most familiarly to understand.

I proceed to give you illustrations of this position, that "Poetry is the indirect expression of that which cannot be expressed directly." An American writer tells us that in a certain town in America there is a statue of a sleeping boy, which is said to produce a singular feeling of repose in all who gaze on it; and the history of that statue, he says, is this: The sculptor gazed upon the skies on a summer's morning, which had arisen as serene and calm as the blue eternity out of which it came; he went about haunted with the memory of that repose—it was a necessity to him to express it. Had he been a poet, he would have thrown it into words; a painter, it would have found expression on the canvas; had he been an architect, he would have given us his feelings embodied as the builders of the Middle Ages embodied their aspirations, in a Gothic architecture; but being a sculptor, his pen was the chisel, his words stone, and so he threw his thoughts into the marble. Now observe, first, this was intense feeling longing to express itself;

next, it was intense feeling expressing itself indirectly, direct utterance being denied it. It was not enough to *say*, "I feel repose;" infinitely more was to be said; more than any words could exhaust: the only material through which he could shape it, and give to airy nothing a body and a form, was the imperfectly expressive material of stone.

From this anecdote we may understand in what sense all the high arts, such as Sculpture, Painting, and Poetry, have been called imitative arts. There was no resemblance between the sleeping boy and a calm morning; but there was a resemblance between the *feeling* produced by the morning, and that produced by gazing on the statue. And it is in this resemblance between the feeling conceived by the artist, and the feeling produced by his work, that the imitation of Poetry or Art lies. The fruit which we are told was painted by the ancient artist so well that the birds came and pecked at it, and the curtain painted by his rival so like reality that he himself was deceived by it, were imitative so far as clever deception imitates; but it was not high art, any more than the statue which many of you saw in the Exhibition last year was high art, which at a distance seemed covered with a veil, but on nearer approach turned out to be mere deceptive resemblance of the texture, cleverly executed in stone. This is not the poetry of Art; it is only the imitation of one species of material in another species; whereas Poetry is the imitating, by suggestion through material and form, of feelings which are immaterial and formless.

Another instance. At Blenheim, the seat of the Duke of Marlborough, there is a Madonna, into which the old Catholic painter has tried to cast the religious conceptions of the Middle Ages, virgin purity and infinite repose. The look is upwards, the predominant colour of the picture blue, which we know has in itself a strange power to lull and soothe. It is impossible to gaze on this picture without being conscious of a calming influence. During that period of the year in which the friends of the young men of Oxford come to visit their brothers and sons, and Blenheim becomes a place of favourite resort, I have stood aside near that picture, to watch its effect on the different gazers, and I have seen group after group of young undergraduates and ladies, full of life and noisy spirits, unconsciously stilled before it; the countenance relaxing into calmness, and the voice sinking to a whisper. The painter had spoken his message, and human beings, ages after, feel what he meant to say.

You may perhaps have seen in this town, some

years ago, an engraving in the windows of the printsellers, called the "Camel of the Desert." I cannot say it was well executed. The engraving was coarse, and the drawing, in some points, false; yet it was full of Poetry. The story tells itself. A caravan has passed through the desert; one of the number has been seized with dangerous illness, and as time is precious, he has been left to die, but as there is a chance of his recovery, his camel has been left beside him, and in order that it may not escape, the knee of the animal has been forcibly bent, the upper and lower bones tied together, and the camel couched on the ground incapable of rising. The sequel is that the man has died, and the camel is left to its inevitable doom. There is nothing to break the deep deathfulness of the scene. The desert extends to the horizon, without interruption, the glowing heat being shown by the reflection of the sun from the sands in a broad band of light, just as it glows on the sea on a burning summer day.

Nothing, I said, breaks the deathfulness of the scene; there is only one thing that adds to it. A long line of vultures is seen in the distance, and one of these loathsome birds is hovering above the dead and the doomed; the camel bends back his neck to watch it, with an expression of terror and anguish almost human, and anticipates its doom. You cannot look at the print without a vivid sense and conception of Despair. You go through street after street before the impression ceases to haunt you. Had the plate been better executed, it is quite possible it might not have been so poetical. The very rudeness and vagueness of it leave much to the imagination. Had the plumage of the vulture, or the hair of the camel more accurately copied the living texture, or the face of the corpse been more deathlike, so as, instead of kindling the imagination with the leading idea, to have drawn away the attention to the fidelity with which the accessories had been painted, the Poetry would have been lessened. It is the effort to express a feeling, and the obstacles in the way of the expression, which together constitute the poetical.

Most of us visited the Exhibition in Hyde Park, last year. Some may have seen between the central fountain and the Colebrook Dale gates several cases of stuffed birds, and probably passed on after a cursory glance. If so, it was a pity, for there was much Poetry in those cases. They contained a series illustrative of falconry.* In the first case was a gyr-falcon, hooded; in the second, the falcon has struck his quarry, and the

* Contributed to the Exhibition by Mr. Hancock, of Newcastle-upon-Tyne.

heron lies below with ruffled crest, and open beak, and writhing, serpentine neck, the falcon meanwhile fixing his talons deep, and throwing himself backwards with open wings to avoid the formidable beak. In the third, the falcon sits gorged upon its perch.

I have visited the finest museums in Europe, and spent many a long day in watching the habits of birds in the woods, hidden and unseen by them; but I never saw the reproduction of life till I saw these. It was not merely the exquisite arrangement of the feathers, nor merely that the parts which are usually dry and shrunk in preserved specimens, the beak and the orbits, the tongue and the legs, were preserved with a marvellous freshness; it was not the mere softness of every swell, and the graceful rise and bend wherever rise and bend should be, but it was the life and feeling thrown into the whole, that dignified these works as real Art. They were vitalized by the feeling, not of the mere bird-stuffer, but of the poet, who had sympathized with nature, felt the life in birds as something kindred with his own; and inspired with this sympathy, and labouring to utter it, had thus re-created life as it were within the very grasp of death.

And while on this subject, I may give you another illustration, by which you will perceive the difference between Science and Poetry, in the works, if you have ever time to read them, published in a cheap form, of Wilson, the American ornithologist. Wilson was born at Paisley; his first poetic inspiration came from the perusal of the works of his countryman, Burns. He emigrated to America, and there devoted his life to ornithology. He studied the life of birds in their native haunts, and the result was a work which stands amongst the foremost in its own department, and which one of the greatest ornithologists of the day, Prince Lucien Bonaparte, has felt it an honour to arrange scientifically. Wilson's enthusiasm and imaginative temperament are manifested in the singular wish that when he died he might be buried in the woods, where the birds would sing above his grave. And all his writing is full of this living sympathy with life, and poetic power of perceiving analogies: as when he calls the Arctic Owl "that great northern Hunter," or describes the Goat-sucker's discovery of the robbery of her nest. Whoever has read his works, or Waterton's Wanderings, or that sweet, observing description given by Banquo, in Macbeth, of the swallow's haunts and dispositions, and will compare the aspect in which life appeared to them with that in which it presents itself to the mind of the scientific nomenclator, will understand the different ways in which Intellect and Feeling represent the same objects, and how it is that largeness of sympathy distinguishes poetic sensibility from scientific capacity. Poetry creates life; Science dissects death.

Our present definition will help to explain why all the scenes of nature are poetic and dear to us. They express what is in us, and what we cannot express for ourselves. I love those passages in the Bible which speak of this universe as created by the WORD of God. For the Word is the expression of the thought; and the visible universe is the Thought of the Eternal, uttered in a word or form in order that it might be intelligible to man. And for an open heart and a seeing eye it is impossible to gaze on this creation without feeling that there is a Spirit at work, a living WORD endeavouring to make himself intelligible, *labouring* to express himself through symbolism and indirect expression, because direct utterance is impossible; partly on account of the inadequacy of the materials, and partly in consequence of the dulness of the heart, to which the infinite Love is speaking. And thus the word poet obtains its literal significance of maker, and all visible things become to us the chaunted poem of the universe.

These feelings, of course, come upon us most vividly in what we call the sublime scenes of nature. I wish I could give to the Working Men in this room one conception of what I have seen and witnessed, or bring the emotions of those glorious spots to the hearts of those who cannot afford to see them. I wish I could describe one scene, which is passing before my memory this moment, when I found myself alone in a solitary valley of the Alps, without a guide, and a thunder-storm coming on; I wish I could explain how every circumstance combined to produce the same feeling, and ministered to unity of impression: the slow, wild wreathing of the vapours round the peaks, concealing their summits, and imparting in semblance their own motion, till each dark mountain form seemed to be mysterious and alive; the eagle-like plunge of the Lämmer-geier, the bearded vulture of the Alps; the rising of the flock of choughs, which I had surprised at their feast on carrion, with their red beaks and legs, and their wild shrill cries, startling the solitude and silence,—till the blue lightning streamed at last, and the shattering thunder crashed as if the mountains must give way: and then came the feelings, which in their fulness man can feel but once in life; mingled sensations of awe and triumph, and defiance of danger, pride, rapture, contempt of pain, humbleness and intense repose, as if all the strife and struggle of the elements were only uttering the unrest of man's bosom; so that in all such scenes there is a feeling of relief, and he is tempted to cry out exultingly, There! there! all this was in my heart, and it was never said out till now!

But do not fancy that Poetry belongs to the grander scenes of nature only. The poets have taught us that throughout the whole world there is a significance as deep as that which belongs to the more startling forms, through which Power speaks.

Burns will show you the Poetry of the daisy,

> "Wee, modest, crimson-tippit flower,"

which the plough turns up unmarked; and Tennyson will tell you the significance, and feeling, and meaning there are in the black ash-bud, and the crumpled poppy, and the twinkling laurels, and the lights which glitter on the panes of the gardener's greenhouse, and the moated grange, and the long, gray flats of "unpoetic" Lincolnshire. Read Wordsworth's "Nutting," and his fine analysis of the remorse experienced in early youth at the wanton tearing down of branches, as if the desolation on which the blue sky looks reproachfully through the open space where foliage was before, were a crime against life, and you will feel the intuitive truth of his admonition that "there is a Spirit in the woods."

Nay, even round this Brighton of ours, treeless and prosaic as people call it, there are materials enough for Poetry, for the heart that is not petrified in conventional maxims about beauty. Enough in its free downs, which are ever changing their distance and their shape, as the lights and cloud-shadows sail over them, and over the graceful forms of whose endless variety of slopes the eye wanders, unarrested by abruptness, with an entrancing feeling of fulness, and a restful satisfaction to the pure sense of Form. And enough upon our own sea-shore and in our rare sunsets. A man might have watched with delight, beyond all words, last night, the long, deep purple lines of cloud, edged with intolerable radiance, passing into orange, yellow, pale green, and leaden blue, and reflected below in warm, purple shadows, and cold, green lights, upon the sea—and then, the dying of it all away? And then he might have remembered those lines of Shakspeare; and often quoted as they are, the poet would have interpreted the sunset, and the sunset what the poet meant by the exclamation which follows the disappearance of a similar aërial vision—

"We are such stuff
As dreams are made of: and our narrow life
Is rounded with a sleep."

No one has taught us this so earnestly as Wordsworth; for it was part of his great message to this century to remind us that the sphere of the poet is not only in the extraordinary, but in the ordinary and common.

"The common things of sky and earth,
And hill and valley, he has viewed:
And impulses of deeper birth
Have come to him in solitude.

"From common things, that round us lie,
Some random truths he can impart:
The harvest of a quiet eye,
That sleeps and broods on its own heart."

But, of course, if you lead a sensual life, or a mercenary or artificial life, you will not read these truths in nature. The faculty of discerning them is not learnt either in the gin-palace or the ball-room. A pure heart, and a simple, manly life alone can reveal to you all that which seer and poet saw.

This Lecture will be appropriately closed by a brief notice of the last work of our chief living poet, Alfred Tennyson. And I shall also endeavour to confute certain cavils raised against it: for after laying down what appear to be true canons of criticism, they may be further substantiated by the exposure of criticism which is false.

The poem entitled "In Memoriam" is a monument erected by friendship to the memory of a gifted son of the historian Hallam. It is divided into a number of cabinet-like compartments, which, with fine and delicate shades of difference, exhibit the various phases through which the bereaved spirit passes from the first shock of despair, dull, hopeless misery and rebellion, up to the dawn of hope, acquiescent trust, and even calm happiness again. In the meanwhile many a question has been solved, which can only suggest itself when suffering forces the soul to front the realities of our mysterious existence; such as: Is there indeed a life to come? And if there is, will it be a conscious life? Shall I know that myself? Will there be mutual recognition? continuance of attachments? Shall friend meet friend, and brother brother, as friends and brothers? Or, again: How comes it that one so gifted was taken away so early, in the maturity of his powers, just at the moment when they seemed about to become available to mankind? What means all this, and is there not something wrong? Is the law of Creation Love indeed?

By slow degrees, all these doubts, and worse, are answered; not as a philosopher would answer them, nor as a theologian, or a metaphysician, but as it is the duty of a poet to reply, by intuitive faculty, in strains in which Imagination predominates over Thought and Memory. And one of the manifold beauties of this exquisite poem, and which is another characteristic of true Poetry, is that, piercing through all the sophistries and over-refinements of speculation, and the lifeless skepticism of science, it falls back upon the grand, primary, simple truths of our humanity; those first principles which underlie all creeds, which belong to our earliest childhood, and on which the wisest and best have rested through all ages; that all is right; that darkness shall be clear; that God and Time are the only interpreters: that Love is king: that the Immortal is in us: that—which is the key-note of the whole—

"all is well, though Faith and Form
Be sundered in the night of fear."

This is an essential quality of the highest Poetry, whose characteristic is simplicity; not in the sense of being intelligible, like a novel, to every careless reader, without pain or effort; for the best Poetry demands study as severe as mathematics require; and to any one who thinks that it can be treated as a mere relaxation and amusement for an idle hour, this Lecture does not address itself; but simplicity, in the sense of dealing with truths which do not belong to a few fastidious and refined intellects, but are the heritage of the many. The deepest truths are the simplest and the most common.

It is wonderful how generally the formalists have missed their way to the interpretation of this poem. It is sometimes declared with oracular decisiveness, that, if this be Poetry, all they have been accustomed to call Poetry must change its name. As if it were not a law that every original poet must be in a sense new; as if Æschylus were not a poet because he did not write an epic like Homer: or as if the Romantic poets were not poets because they departed from every rule of classical Poetry. And as if, indeed, this very objection had not been brought against the Romantic school, and Shakspeare himself pronounced by French critics a "buffoon:" till Schlegel showed that all life makes to itself its own form, and that Shakspeare's form had its living laws. So spoke the "Edinburgh Review" of Byron; but it could not arrest his career. So spoke Byron himself of Wordsworth; but he would be a bold man, or a very flippant one, who would dare to say now that Wordsworth is not a great poet. And the day will come when the slow, sure judgment of Time shall give to Tennyson his undisputed place among the English poets as a true one, of rare merit and originality.

To a coarser class of minds "In Memoriam" appears too melancholy; one long monotone of grief. It is simply one of the most victorious songs that ever poet chaunted; with the mysterious undertone, no doubt, of sadness which belongs to all human joy, in front of the mysteries of death and sorrow; but that belongs to "Paradise Regained" as well as to "Paradise Lost;" to every true note, indeed, of human triumph except a Bacchanalian drinking song. And that it should predominate in a monumental record is not particularly unnatural. But readers who never dream of mastering the plan of a work before they pretend to criticize details, can scarcely be expected to perceive that the wail passes into a hymn of solemn and peaceful beauty before it closes.

Another objection, proceeding from the religious periodicals, is, that the subject being a religious one, is not treated religiously; by which they mean theologically. It certainly is neither saturated with Evangelicalism nor Tractarianism; nor does it abound in the routine phrases which, when missed, raise a suspicion of heterodoxy; nor does it seize the happy opportunity afforded for a pious denunciation of the errors of

Purgatory and Mariolatry. But the objection to its want of definite theology—an objection, by the way, brought frequently against Wordsworth by writers of the same school—is, in fact, in favour of the presumption of its poetic merit; for it may be the office of the priest to teach upon authority—of the philosopher according to induction—but the province of the poet is neither to teach by induction nor by authority, but to appeal to those primal intuitions of our being which are eternally and necessarily true.

With one of those criticisms I mean to occupy your time at somewhat further length. Some months ago, a leading journal devoted three or four columns to the work of depreciating Tennyson. I will answer that critique now, as concisely as I can; not because it can do any permanent harm to Tennyson's reputation, but because it may do a great deal of harm to the taste of the readers.

Now, in any pretension to criticize a poetic work of internal unity, the first duty, plainly, is to comprehend the structure of it as a whole, and master the leading idea. It is to be regretted that this is precisely what English critics generally do not. Even with our own Shakspeare, admiration or blame is usually confined to the beauties and blemishes of detached passages.

For the significance of each play, as a whole, we had to look, in the first instance, to such foreigners as Augustus Schlegel to teach us.

Let us inquire what conception the critic in question has formed of this beautiful poem.

"Let the acknowledgment be made at once that the writer dedicated his thoughts to a most difficult task. He has written 200 pages upon one person—in other words, he has painted 120 miniatures of the same individual."

Mr. Tennyson has not painted 120 portraits of the same individual. He has written a poem in 120 divisions, illustrative of the manifold phases through which the soul passes from doubt through grief to faith. With so entire and radical a misconception of the scope of the poem, it is not wonderful if the whole examination of the details should be a failure.

The first general charge is one of irreverence. The special case selected is these verses, which are called blasphemous—

"But brooding on the dear one dead,
And all he said of things divine,
(And dear as sacramental wine
To dying lips is all he said.)"

One would have thought that the holy tenderness of this passage would have made this charge impossible. However, as notions of reverence and irreverence in some minds are singularly vague, we will give the flippant objection rather more attention than it merits.

By a sacrament we understand a means of grace; an outward something through which pure and holy feelings are communicated to the soul. In the Church of Christ there are two sacraments—the material of one is the commonest of all elements, water; the form of the other the commonest of all acts, a meal. Now there are two ways in which reverence may be manifested towards any thing or person; one, by exalting that thing or person by means of the depreciation of all others; another, by exalting all others through it. To some minds it appears an honouring of the sacraments to represent them as solitary things in their own kind, like nothing else, and all other things and acts profane in comparison of them. It is my own deep conviction that no greater dishonour can be done to them than by this conception, which degrades them to the rank of charms. The sacraments are honoured when they consecrate all the things and acts of life. The commonest of all materials was sanctified to us in order to vindicate the sacredness of all materialism, in protest against the false spiritualism which affects to despise the body, and the world whose impressions are made upon the senses; and in order to declare that visible world God's, and the organ of his manifestation. The simplest of all acts is sacramental, in order to vindicate God's claim to all acts, and to proclaim our common life sacred, in protest against the conception which cleaves so obstinately to the mind, that religion is the performance of certain stated acts, not necessarily of moral import, on certain days and in certain places. If there be any thing in this life sacred, any remembrance filled with sanctifying power, any voice which symbolizes to us the voice of God, it is the recollection of the pure and holy ones that have been taken from us, and of their examples and sacred words—

> "dear as sacramental wine
> To dying lips."

In those lines Tennyson has deeply, no doubt unconsciously, that is, without dogmatic intention, entered into the power of the sacraments to diffuse their meaning beyond themselves. There is no irreverence in them; no blasphemy; nothing but delicate Christian truth.

The next definite charge is more difficult to deal with before a mixed society, because the shades of the feeling in question blend into each other with exceeding fine graduation. The language of the friend towards the departed friend is represented as unfitted for any but amatory tenderness. In this blame the critic is compelled to include Shakspeare; for we all know that his sonnets, dedicated either to the Earl of Southampton or the Earl of Pembroke, contain expressions which have left it a point of controversy whether they were addressed to a lady or a friend. Now in a matter which concerns the truthfulness of a human feeling, when an anonymous critic is on one side and Shakspeare on the other, there are some who might be presumptuous enough to suppose *à priori* that the modest critic is possibly not the one in the right. However, let us examine the matter. There are two kinds of friendship: One is the affection of the greater for the less, the other that of the less for the greater. The greater and the less may be differences of rank, or intellect, or character, or power. These are the two opposites of feeling which respectively characterize the masculine and the feminine natures, the familiar symbols of which relationship are the oak and the ivy with its clinging tendrils. But though they are the masculine and feminine types, they are not confined to male and female. Most of us have gone through both these phases of friendship. Whoever remembers an attachment at school to a boy feebler than himself, will recollect the exulting pride of guardianship with which he shielded his friend from the oppression of some young tyrant of the playground. And whoever, at least in boyhood or youth, loved a man, to whose mental or moral qualities he looked up with young reverence, will recollect the devotion and the jealousies, and the almost passionate tenderness, and the costly gifts, and the desire of personal sacrifices, which characterize boyish friendship, and which certainly belong to the feminine, and not the masculine type of affection. Doubtless the language of "In Memoriam" is tender in the extreme, such as a sister might use to a brother deeply loved. But it is to be remembered that it expresses the affection of the spirit which rejoices to confess itself the feebler; and besides, that, the man has passed into a spirit, and that time and distance have thrown a hallowing haze of tenderness over the lineaments of the friend of the past. It may be well also to recollect that there is a precedent for this woman-like tenderness, against whose authority one who condemns so severely the most distant approach to irreverence will scarcely venture to appeal. "I am distressed for thee, my brother Jonathan; very pleasant hast thou been to me. Thy love to me was wonderful, *passing the love of women.*"

Again, the praise and the grief of the poem are enormously "exaggerated;" and as an instance of the manner in which the "*poet* may underline the moralist," and delicately omit the defects without hyperbolical praise, Dr. Johnson's lines on Levett are cited with much fervour of admiration. Good, excellent Dr. Johnson! sincerely pious; very bigoted and very superstitious; yet one, withal, who fought the battle of life bravely out, in the teeth of disease and poverty; a great lexicographer; of massive learning; the author of innumerable prudential aphorisms, much quoted by persons who season their conversation with proverbs and old saws; the inditer of several thousand ponderous verses; a man worthy of all respect. But it is indeed a surprising apparition when the shade of Dr. Johnson descends upon the Nineteenth Century as the spirit of a poet, and we are asked to identify the rugged portrait which Boswell painted, with a model of delicate forbearance.

After these general observations, the writer proceeds to criticize in detail; he awards some praise, and much blame. You shall have a specimen of each. Let us test the value of his praise. He selects for approbation, among others, these lines:

"Or is it that the Past will win
A glory from its being far;
And orb into the perfect star
We saw not when we moved therein!"

The question has suggested itself as a misgiving to the poet's mind, whether his past affection was really as full of blessedness as memory painted it, or whether it be not the perspective of distance which conceals its imperfections, and throws purer hues upon it than it possessed while actual. In the rapid reading of the last two lines I may not have at once conveyed to you the meaning. So long as we remain upon any planet, this earth for instance, it would wear a common-place, earthly look; but if we could ascend from it into space, in proportion to the distance, it would assume a heavenly aspect, and orb or round itself into a star. This is a very simple and graceful illustration. Now hear the critic condescending to be an analyst of its beauties:

"There is indeed something striking and suggestive in comparing the gone-by time to some luminous body rising like a red harvest moon behind us, lighting our path homeward."

So that this beautiful simile of Tennyson's, of a distant star receding into pale and perfect loveliness, in the hands of the critic becomes *a great red harvest moon!*

So much for the praise. Now for the blame. The following passage is selected:—

"Oh, if indeed that eye foresee,
Or see (in Him is no before)
In more of life true love no more,
And love the indifference to be,

"So might I find, ere yet the morn
Breaks hither over Indian seas,
That Shadow waiting with the keys,
To cloak me from my proper scorn."

That is, as you will see at once, after the thought of the transitoriness of human affection has occurred to him, the possibility is also suggested with it, that he himself may change; but he prays that before that day can come, he may find the Shadow waiting with the keys to cloak him from his own scorn. Now I will read the commentary:—

"Lately we have heard much of keys, both from the Flaminian Gate and Piccadilly, but we back this verse against Hobbs. We dare him to pick it. Mr. Moxon may hang it up in his window, with a 200*l.* prize attached, more safely than a Brahmah. That a shadow should hold keys at all, is a noticeable circumstance; but that it should wait with a cloak, ready to be thrown over a gentleman in difficulties, is absolutely amazing."

The lock may be picked without any exertion of unfair force.

A few pages before he has spoken of the breaking up of a happy friendship—

> "There sat the Shadow, feared by man,
> Who broke our fair companionship."

Afterward he calls it:—

> "The Shadow, cloaked from head to foot,
> Who keeps the key of all the creeds."

Take, at a venture, any charity-school boy, of ordinary intelligence; read to him these lines; and he will tell you that the Shadow feared by man is death; that it is cloaked from head to foot because death is mysterious, and its form not distinguishable; and that he keeps the keys of all the creeds, because he alone can unlock the secret of the grave, and show which of all conflicting human creeds is true.

"It is a noticeable thing," we are told, "that a shadow should hold keys at all." It is a very noticeable thing that a skeleton should hold a scythe and an hour-glass; very noticeable that a young lady should hold scales when she is blindfold; yet it is not a particularly uncommon rule of symbolism so to represent Time and Justice. Probably the writer in the criticism, if he should chance to read of "riding on the wings of the wind," would consider it a very noticeable method of locomotion; perhaps would inquire, with dull facetiousness, what was the precise length of the primary, secondary, and tertiary quills of the said wings; and if told of a spirit clothing itself in light, he might triumphantly demand in what loom light could be woven into a great coat.

Finally. The critique complains that a vast deal of poetic feeling has been wasted on a lawyer; and much wit is spent upon the tenderness which is given to "Amaryllis of the Chancery bar." A barrister, it seems, is beyond the pale of excusable, because political sensibilities. So that, if my friend be a soldier, I may love him, and celebrate him in poetry, because the profession of arms is by all conventional associations heroic; or if he bears on his escutcheon the red hand of knighthood, or wears a ducal coronet, or even be a shepherd, still there are poetic precedents for romance; but if he be a member of the Chancery bar, or only a cotton lord, then, because these are not yet grades accredited as heroic in song, worth is not worth, and honour is not honour, and nobleness is not nobility. O, if we wanted poets for nothing else, it would be for this, that they are the grand levellers, vindicating the sacredness of our common humanity, and in protest against such downright vulgarity of heart as this, reminding us that—

> "For a' that, and a' that,
> A man's a man for a' that."

So much then for this critic; wrong when he praises and wrong when he blames; who finds Shakspeare false to the facts of human nature, and quotes Dr. Johnson as a model poet; who cannot believe in the Poetry of any expression unless it bear the mint-stamp of a precedent, and cannot understand either the exaggerations or the infinitude of genuine grief.

Let it serve to the members of this Institution as a comment on the opinion quoted at the outset, that it is sufficient education for Working Men to read the newspapers. If they form no more living conception of what Poetry is than such as they get from the flippant criticism of a slashing article, they may learn satire, but not enthusiasm. If they limit their politics to the knowledge they may pick up from daily newspapers (which, with a few honourable exceptions, seem bound to pander to all the passions and prejudices of their respective factions) they will settle down into miserable partizans. And if Working Men are to gain their notions of Christianity from the sneering, snarling gossip of the religious newspapers, I for one, do not marvel that indignant infidelity is so common amongst them.

And let it be to us all a warning against that detracting, depreciating spirit which is the curse and bane both of the religion and the literature of our day—that spirit which has no sympathy with aught that is great beyond the pale of customary formalities, and sheds its blighting influence over all that is enthusiastic, and generous, and high-minded. It is possible for a sneer or a cavil to strike sometimes a superficial fact; I never knew the one or the other reach the deep heart and blessedness of truth.

LECTURE II.

IN the former Lecture I endeavoured to answer the question—What is Poetry? Two replies were given: It is the natural language of excited feeling; and—A work of imagination wrought into form by art. We said that it arises out of the necessity of expression, and the impossibility of adequate expression of any of the deeper feelings in direct terms. Hence the soul clothes those feelings in symbolic and sensuous imagery, in order to *suggest* them.

And thus our definitions agree with two of Milton's requirements for Poetry—that it be "simple, sensuous, passionate." Sensuous, that is, suggestive to the imagination of truth through images which make their impression on the senses. Passionate, that is, as opposed to scientific; for the province of Poetry is not the intellect, but the feelings.

And thus, too, they coincide with the character

given to Poetry by the great critic of antiquity, as an imitative art; for it is the art of suggesting and thus imitating through form, the feelings that have been suggested by another form, or perhaps have arisen without form at all. So it takes its place with all art, whose office is not to copy form by form, but to express and hint spiritual truths.

It is plain, from what has been said, that Poetry may be spoken of in two senses. In the specific or technical sense, by Poetry we mean the expression in words, most appropriately metrical words, of the truths of imagination and feeling. But in the generic and larger sense, Poetry is the expression of imaginative truth in any form, provided only that it be symbolic, suggestive, and indirect. Hence we said that there is a Poetry of sculpture, architecture, painting; and hence all nature is poetical, because it is the form in which the eternal Feeling has clothed itself with infinite suggestiveness: and hence Lord Byron calls the stars "the Poetry of heaven;" and tells us that to him "high mountains were a feeling;" and that mountain and wood and sky spake

"A mutual language, clearer than the tome
Of his land's tongue, which he would oft forsake
For Nature's pages, glassed by sunbeams on the lake."

And hence Wordsworth tells us that Liberty has two voices:

> "One is of the sea,
> And one is of the mountains."

And hence a greater than either has said that the Heavens speak, and that "There is neither speech nor language where their voices are not heard." And hence, too, Woman has been called the Poetry of life, because her presence in this lower world expresses for us, as well as calls out, those infinite feelings of purity, tenderness, and devotion, whose real existence is in our own bosoms. And hence, again, there is a Poetry in music; not in that in which sound imitates sound, as when the roaring of the sea, or the pattering of the rain, or church bells, or bugles, or the groans of the dying are produced, for in such cases there is only a mimicry, more or less ingenious; but that in which we can almost fancy that there is something analogous to the inner history of the human heart,—an expression of resolve or moral victory, or aspiration, or other feelings far more shadowy, infinite, and intangible; or that in which the feelings of a nation have found for themselves an indirect and almost unconscious utterance, as it is said of the Irish melody, that through it, long centuries of depression have breathed themselves out in cadences of a wild, low wail.

We divided poets into two orders: those in whom the vision and the faculty divine of imagination exists; and those in whom the plastic power of shaping predominates;—the men of poetic inspiration, and the men of poetic taste. In the first order I placed Tennyson; in the second, Pope.

Considerable discussion, I am told, has been excited among the men of this Institution by both these positions,—some warmly defending them, and others as warmly impugning. For myself, it is an abundant reward to find that Working Men can be interested in such questions;—that they can debate the question whether Pope was a poet, and be induced to read Tennyson. For the true aim of every one who aspires to be a teacher is, or ought to be, not to impart his own opinions, but to kindle other minds. I care very little, comparatively, whether you adopt my views or not; but I do care much to know that I can be the humble instrument, in this or higher matters, of leading any man to stir up the power within him, and to form a creed and faith which are in a living way, and not on mere authority, his own.

However, I will explain to you on what grounds I made these two assertions. And, first, as respects Pope—if any one approved of what

I said, under the impression that I denied to Pope the name of poet, I must disclaim his approbation; I did not say so. Pope is a true poet; in his own order he stands amongst the foremost; only, that order is the second, not the first. In the mastery of his materials, which are words, in the plastic power of expression, he is scarcely surpassed. His melody—I do not say his harmony, which is a much higher thing—is unquestionable. There is no writer from whom so many of those sparkling, epigrammatic sentences, which are the staple commodities of quotation, are introduced into conversation; none who can be read with more pleasure, and even profit. He has always a masculine fancy; more rarely, imagination. But you look in vain for the truths which come from a large heart and a seeing eye; in vain for the "thoughts that breathe and the words that burn;" in vain for those flashes of truth, which, like the lightning in a dark night, make all luminous, open out unsuspected glories of tree and sky and building, interpret us to ourselves, and "body forth the shapes of things unknown;" truths which are almost prophetic. Who has not read his Essay on Man, again and again? And yet it is but the philosophy of Bolingbroke, melodiously expressed in rhyme; whereas the office of Poetry is not to make us think accurately, but feel truly. And his Rape of the Lock, which seems to me the one of all his works that most deserves the name of Poetry, the nearest approach to a creation of the fancy, describes aristocratic society, which is uniform, polished, artificial, and out of which a mightier master of the art than Pope could scarcely have struck the notes of true passion. Moreover, its machinery, the Rosicrucian fancies of sylphs and gnomes, is but machinery, lifeless. If you compare Shakspeare's Ariel or Puck, things alive, preternatural, and yet how natural! with these automatons, you will feel the difference between a living creation and cleverly moved puppet work. Throughout you have thought, not imagination; intellect, not intuition.

I read you last time Pope's estimate of his own art; now, contrast it with the conceptions formed of Poetry by men whom I would place in the first order.

First, let Burns speak. The spirit of Scottish poesy has appeared to him, and given him his commission. She says—

"I saw thee seek the sounding shore,
Delighted with the dashing roar;
Or when the North his fleecy store
Drove through the sky,—
I saw grim Nature's visage hoar,
Struck thy young eye.

"Or when the deep, green-mantled earth,
Warm-cherished ev'ry flow'ret's birth,
And joy and music pouring forth
In every grove,—
I saw thee eye the gen'ral mirth,
With boundless love."

Observe that exquisite account of the true poetic or creative power, which comes from love, the power of sympathy with the happiness of all kinds of being—"I saw thee eye the general mirth *with boundless love!*"

Wordsworth shall speak next. I select his Sonnet to Haydon. You remember poor Haydon's tragic end. He died by his own hand, disappointed because the world had not appreciated nor understood his paintings. It had been well for Haydon had he taken to heart the lesson of these lines, pregnant with manly strength for every one, poet or teacher, who is striving to express deep truths for which the men of his generation are not prepared.

And remark, merely by the way, in this sonnet, Wordsworth's corroboration of the view I have placed before you, that Poetry is a something to which words are the accidental, not by any means the essential form.

"High is our calling, friend! Creative Art,
(Whether the instrument of words she use,

Or pencil pregnant with ethereal hues,)
Demands the service of a mind and heart,
Though sensitive, yet, in their weakest part,
Heroically fashioned—to infuse
Faith in the whispers of the lonely Muse,
While the whole world seems adverse to desert.
And, oh! when Nature sinks, as oft she may,
Through long-lived pressure of obscure distress,
Still to be strenuous for the bright reward,
And in the soul admit of no decay,
Brook no continuance of weak-mindedness—
Great is the glory, for the strife is hard!"

We will next listen to the account given us by Milton, of the conditions under which Poetry is possible,—lofty and majestic, as we should expect from him:—

"This is not to be obtained but by devout prayer to that Eternal Spirit that can enrich with all utterance and knowledge, and sends his seraphim with the hallowed fire of his altar, to touch and purify the lips of whom he pleases. To this must be added industrious and select reading, steady observation, and insight into all seemly and generous acts and affairs."

Tennyson shall close this brief list, with what he thinks the poet's calling:

"The poet in a golden clime was born,
With golden stars above;
Dower'd with the hate of hate, the scorn of scorn,
The love of love."

That is,—the Prophet of Truth receives for his dower the scorn of men in whose breasts scorn dwells; hatred from men who hate; while his reward is in the gratitude and affection of men who seek the truth which they love, more eagerly than the faults which their acuteness can blame.

> "He saw through life and death, through good and ill,
> He saw through his own soul,
> The marvel of the everlasting will,
> An open scroll,
> "Before him lay."

And again:

> "Thus truth was multiplied on truth: the world
> Like one great garden show'd,
> And thro' the wreaths of floating dark upcurled
> Rare sunrise flow'd.
>
> "And Freedom rear'd in that august sunrise,
> Her beautiful, bold brow,
> When rites and forms before his burning eyes
> Melted like snow."

Rare gifts of nature: power to read the "open secret of the universe;" the apostleship of light, truth, liberty; the faculty of discerning the life and meaning which underlie all forms: this is Tennyson's notion of a poet. You have heard the master-spirits discoursing of their art. Now if after these, you turn to Pope's conception again, you will feel there is a descent as into another region. A mighty gulf lies between. It is impossible to place these men in the same order. No man is higher than his own ideal of excellence; it is well if he attains that. Pope reached all he aimed at; he reached no more.

I placed Tennyson in the first order. And this not from any bigoted blindness to his deficiencies and faults, which are many; nor from any Quixotic desire to compare him with the very highest; but because, if the division be a true one which separates poets into the men of genuine passion and men of skill, it is impossible to hesitate in which Tennyson is to be placed. I ranked him with the first order, because with great mastery over his material; words, great plastic power of versification and a rare gift of harmony, he has also Vision or Insight; and because, feeling intensely the great questions of his day, not as a mere man of letters, but as a man, he is to some extent the interpreter of his age, not only in its mysticism, which I tried to show you is the necessary reaction from the rigid formulas of science and the earthliness of an age of work, into the vagueness which belongs to infinitude, but also in his poetic and almost prophetic solution of some of its great questions.

Thus in his Princess, which he calls a "medley," the former half of which is sportive, and the plot almost too fantastic and impossible for criticism, while the latter portion seems too serious for a story so slight and flimsy, he has with exquisite taste disposed of the question which has its burlesque and comic as well as its tragic side, of woman's present place and future destinies. And if any one wishes to see this subject treated with a masterly and delicate hand, in protest alike against the theories which would make her as the man, which she could only be by becoming masculine, not manly, and those which would have her to remain the toy, or the slave, or the slight thing of sentimental and frivolous accomplishment which education has hitherto aimed at making her, I would recommend him to study the few last pages of the Princess, where the poet brings the question back, as a poet should, to nature; developes the ideal out of the actual woman, and reads out of what she is, on the one hand, what her Creator intended her to be, and, on the other, what she never can nor ought to be.

And again, in his "In Memoriam," he has grappled with the skepticism of his age; not like the school-divine, but like a poet; not as a priest, with the thunder of the pulpit, or the ban of the conventicle, but as a man; a man of large, human heart, who feels that not doubt, but faith is greatness and blessedness, yet that doubt must not be put down by force or terror, nor silenced by logic, but pass into belief through sorrow, and by appeal to the intuitions of the Soul.

The severity with which an article written against this poem was criticized in the previous lecture, may have seemed to you more than adequate. Let me explain. Three things only in this world should receive no quarter: Hypocrisy, Pharisaism, and Tyranny. Hypocrisy, of course, is out of the question here. But by Pharisaism in religion, we mean, not attachment to forms, but an incapacity of seeing or believing in goodness separate from some particular form, either of words or ritual. The incipient stage of Pharisaism is that in which men are blind to excellence which does not belong to their own faction; the final and completed stage is that in which goodness seems actually evil. Plainly, there can be no remedy for that; when good is taken for evil, and evil for good, the heart has reached its last rottenness. By Pharisaism in art we mean, not an attachment to particular schools, but an inability of recognizing beauty, except in accordance with conventional rules and established maxims; its incipient stage is when beauty in aberrant types is not felt; its final and hopeless stage is reached when such beauty appears deformity.

Now it was the Pharisaism of that article which appeared to me to deserve no common severity.

Tyranny merits the same treatment. Had it been from a feeble antagonist that this criticism proceeded, it might have been left unnoticed. Who "breaks a butterfly upon a wheel?" Or had it been vulgar, personal slander, it had been met, as all such things are best met, in silence. But the journal in which this critique appeared is no vulgar slanderer; scarcely ever is an article in its columns deficient in talent at least; few would like to writhe beneath its lash. It wields a gigantic power. Well, it is excellent

> "To have a giant's strength; but it is tyrannous
> To use it like a giant."

And because that article was written with merciless severity, weighted with all the authority of a powerful journal, and hidden behind the shelter of an anonymous incognito, therefore it seemed to me a bounden duty to show to Working Men that a giant can be crushed, and that they are not to be led blindfold by the press; inasmuch as even an article in the "leading journal of Europe" may be flippant, clever, arrogant, and shallow.

We proceed to the more direct business of this

evening: the *influence* of Poetry on the Working Classes. But first, I disclaim the notion of treating this subject as if Poetry had a different sort of influence on them from that which it has on other classes. Very false is that mode of thought which recognizes the souls of the classes who are not compelled to work as composed of porcelain, and of those who are doomed to work as made of clay. They feel, weep, laugh, alike; alike have their aspiring and their degraded moods; that which tells on one human spirit, tells also upon another. Much, therefore, of what is to be said will belong to men of work; not specially, but only as human beings. If Poetry influences men, it must influence Working Men.

The influence of Poetry depends partly on the form; and partly on the spirit which animates the form. I will consider the influence of form first.

We have defined Poetry to be a work of imagination wrought into form by art. Poetry is not imagination, but imagination shaped. Not feeling; but feeling expressed symbolically; the formless suggested indirectly through form. Hence the form is an essential element of Poetry; and it becomes necessary to trace its influence.

The form in which poetical feeling expresses itself is infinitely varied. There may be a poetical act, or a poetical picture, or a poetical aspect of scenery, or poetical words; to which last form we technically give the name of Poetry.

Take an example from an expression of countenance, which may be poetical. There are feelings which cannot be spoken out in words; therefore the Creator has so constituted the human countenance that it is expressive, and you only catch the meaning sympathetically by the symbolism of the features. We have all seen such Poetry. We have seen looks inspired. We have seen whole worlds of feeling in a glance; scorn, hatred, devotion, infinite tenderness. This is what, in portraits, we call expression, as distinguished from similarity of feature. Innumerable touches perfect the one; sometimes one masterly stroke will suggest the other, so that nothing can add to it. This is Poetry. To such a look the addition of a word would have spoilt all—

> "For words are weak, and most to seek,
> When wanted fifty-fold:
> And then, if silence will not speak,
> And trembling lip, and changing cheek,
> There's nothing *told*."

The form of Poetry, again, may be that of a symbolical action. The Eastern nations express themselves abundantly in this way; and if the subject were not too sacred, I might adduce many examples from the significant actions of the Hebrew prophets. But I will, instead, instance a case of modern history. Perhaps you have read the anecdote (I do not know on what historical authority it rests) of the Earl of Warwick, in one of his last battles, probably that of Barnet, when he found the day going against him, dismounting from his favourite charger, and before all his army plunging his sword into his heart, thereby cutting off the possibility of escape, and expressing his resolve there to win or fall. Conceive Warwick putting that into direct words. Conceive his attempting to express all that was implied in that act; the energy of despair, the resolve, the infinite defiance, the untold worlds of *force* that must be in a man who could do an act the whole terribleness of which none but a soldier could appreciate, slaying with his own hand the horse and friend that had borne him through death and perils. And conceive the influence upon the troops—how it must have said to any recreant waverer in the ranks, "Stand like a man, and dare to die!"

The next instance is a less dignified one; but I select it that we may discern the manifold shapes and degrees of poetic form. History tells us of a prince of France who asked permission to offer a present to one much loved. The permission was given; the gift chosen, a portrait;

but with a stipulation annexed, in order to prevent extravagance, that it should not be larger than could be worn as a ring upon the finger, and that it should not be set in jewels. The portrait was completed as agreed on; but, instead of a glass, it was covered with a single plate, cut out of the centre of an enormous diamond, which, of course, was sacrificed in the cutting. When the ingenious treachery was discovered, the picture was returned: whereupon the royal lover ground the diamond to powder, and dusted with it, instead of sand, his letter of reply. The use of this? It was useless. Had it been a matter of utility, it had not been one of Poetry. It was modified by French feeling, doubtless. Yet beneath it you will discern something that was not merely French, but human, and which constitutes the Poetry of the whole system of present giving. That which in the polite Frenchman was something more than gallantry, would have been in another, and in him, too, under more earnest or less successful circumstances, the chivalrous feeling which desires to express itself in its true essence, as devotion to the weaker, through a sacrifice which shall be costly, (the costlier the more grateful, as the relief of feeling to the giver,) and which shall be quite immeasurable by, and independent of, the question of utility. The love of the base and plebeian spirit is the desire to *take* all it can. The love of the nobler spirit is the desire to *give* all it can. Sacrifice is its only true expression; and every form of sacrifice in which the soul tries to express and relieve itself, whether it be in the lavish magnificence in which self and life can be freely spent, or the vulgar magnificence called princely, with which gold and jewels can be squandered, is a form of Poetry, more or less dignified.

It will now be clear, that in the large sense of the word Poetry, its proper form is always symbolism. The poet derives his power from the ardour of mankind to adopt symbols, and catch enthusiasm from them. Poetry is the language of symbolism.

Therefore we all are susceptible of its influences. Many a man who thinks he has no taste for Poetry, because he does not chance to feel it in one of its forms, rhythmic words, is yet no stranger to its power. What is religious formalism, but an exaggeration or petrifaction of a true conviction—that outward forms and material symbols have a language of their own, fraught with a deeper, because infinite, religious significance to the heart than ever came from the poor rhetoric of the pulpit? Why is it that on the battle field there is ever one spot where the sabres glitter faster, and the pistol's flash is more frequent, and men and officers crowd together in denser masses? They are struggling for a flag, or an eagle, or a standard. Strip it of its symbolism—take from it the meaning with which the imagination has invested it, and it is nothing but a bit of silk rag, torn with shot and blackened with powder. Now go with your common sense and tell the soldier he is madly striving about a bit of rag. See if your common sense is as true to him as his Poetry, or able to quench it for a moment.

Take a case. Among the exploits of marvellous and almost legendary valour performed by that great Chieftain, to whom not many years ago, when disaster after disaster left it uncertain whether the next mail would bring us news that we possessed any Indian Empire at all, the voice of England, with one unanimous impulse, cried, "There is one man in Britain who has the right of wisdom as well as courage to command in chief,"—that daring warrior who, when the hour of danger was past, and the hour of safety had come, was forgotten by his country; to whom in the hour of fresh danger the people of England will look again, and his generous spirit will forget neglect; who has been laid aside uncoroneted and almost unhonoured, because he *would* promote and distinguish the men of work in preference to the men of rank, and wealth, and titled idleness—amongst his achievements not the least wondrous was his subjugation of the robber tribes of the Cutchee hills, in the North of Scinde. Those warriors had been unsubdued for six hundred years. They dwelt in a crater-like valley, surrounded by mountains, through which there were but two or three narrow entrances, and up which there was no access but by goat-paths, so precipitous that brave men grew dizzy and could not proceed. So rude and wild was the fastness of Trukkee, that the entrances themselves could scarcely be discovered amidst the labyrinth-like confusion of rocks and mountains. It was part of the masterly plan by which Sir Charles Napier had resolved to storm the stronghold of the robbers, to cause a detachment of his army to scale the mountain side. A service so perilous could scarcely be commanded. Volunteers were called for. There was a regiment, the 64th Bengal Infantry, which had been recently disgraced, in consequence of mutiny at Shikarpoor, their colonel cashiered, and their colours taken from them —a hundred of these men volunteered. "Soldiers of the 64th," said the commander, who knew the way to the soldier's heart, "your colours are on the top of yonder hill!" I should like to have seen the precipice that would have deterred the 64th regiment, after words like those from the lips of the conqueror of Scinde!

And now, suppose that you had gone with common-sense and economic science, and proved to them that the colours they were risking their lives to win back, were worth but so many shillings sterling value—tell me, which would the stern workers of the 64th regiment have found it easiest to understand, common-sense or Poetry? Which would they have believed, Science, which said, "It is manufactured silk;" or Imagination, whose kingly voice had made it "colours"?

It is in this sense that the poet has been called as the name imports, creator, namer, maker. He stamps his own feeling on a form or symbol; names it, and makes it what it was not before; giving to feeling a local habitation and a name, by associating it with form. Before, it was silk—so many square feet; now, it is a thing for which men will die.

And here we get at two distinctions—

First, between the poet and the rhymester. A poet is one who creates or names; who interprets old or new thoughts by fresh symbolism. The rhymester repeats the accredited forms and phrases; and because he has got the knack of using metaphors and diction, which have been the living language of the makers of them, he is mistaken for a poet. Smooth writing, and facility of versification, and expertness in piecing together poetical words and images, do not constitute Poetry.

Next, a distinction between the poet and the mystic. The poet uses symbols, knowing that they are symbols. The mystic mistakes them for realities. Thus to Swedenborg a cloud, or a vine, or a cedar, correspond throughout Scripture with one mystic spiritual truth; mean one thing, and but one. And thus to the mystical formalist, a sign or symbol is confused with the truth which it symbolizes; that symbol is *the* symbol of that truth; and to treat the symbol as Hezekiah treated the brazen serpent is sacrilege. Now, the poet remains sane upon this point; his "fine frenzy" never reaches the insanity which mistakes its own creations for fixed realities. To him a cloud or flower may express at different times a thousand truths; material things are types to him, in a certain mood, of this truth or that; but he knows that to another person, or to himself in another mood, they are types of something else.

Tennyson has said this well—

> "But any man who walks the mead,
> In bud, or blade, or bloom may find,

According as his humours lead,
A meaning suited to his mind.
For liberal applications lie
In Art as Nature, dearest friend :
So 'twere to cramp its use, if I
Should hook it to some useful end.

And this will help us to discern how far there is truth in the opinion that Poetry belongs to the earlier ages, and declines with the advance of civilization. Symbols perish—Poetry never dies. There was a time when the Trojan war, before Homer sang it, was what Milton says of the unsung wars of the Saxon Heptarchy, a conflict of kites and crows; the martyr's stake, a gibbet; Olympus and Parnassus, and a hill more holy still, common hills. The time may come when, as they were once without poetical associations, most of them shall be unpoetical again. And because of such a dying of the glory from the past, people begin to fancy that Poetry has perished. But is human courage lost, fidelity, imagination, honourable aims? Is the necessity of utterance gone, or the sufficiency of finite words for illimitable feeling greater? When the old colours of a regiment are worn out, it is sometimes the custom to burn them, and drink the ashes in wine, with solemn silence, before the consecration of new colours. Well, that is all we want. Let old forms and time-honoured words perish with due honour, and give us fresh symbols and new forms of speech to express, not what our fathers felt, but what we feel. Goëthe says, "The spirit-world is not foreclosed. *Thy* senses are dulled; *thy* heart is dead. Arise, become a learner; and bathe that earthly breast of thine, unwearied, in the dew of a fresh morning."

And this alone would be enough to show that the Poetry of the coming age must come from the Working Classes. In the upper ranks, Poetry, so far at least as it represents their life, has long been worn out, sickly, and sentimental. Its manhood is effete. Feudal aristocracy with its associations, the castle and the tournament, has passed away. Its last healthy tones came from the harp of Scott. Byron sang its funeral dirge. But tenderness, and heroism, and endurance still want their voice, and it must come from the classes whose observation is at first hand, and who speak fresh from Nature's heart. What has Poetry to do with the Working Classes? Men of work! we want our Poetry from you—from men who will dare to live a brave and true life; not like poor Burns, who was fevered with flattery, manful as he was, and dazzled by the vulgar splendours of the life of the great, which he despised and still longed for; but rather like Ebenezer Elliot, author of the Corn Law Rhymes. Our soldier ancestors told you the significance of high devotion and loyalty which lay beneath the smoke of battle-fields. Now rise and tell us the living meaning there may be in the smoke of manufactories, and the heroism of perseverance, and the poetry of invention, and the patience of uncomplaining resignation. Remember the stirring words of one of your own poets:

> "There's a light about to break,
> There's a day about to dawn:
> Men of thought, and men of action!
> Clear the way!"

Consider, next, the influence of the spirit of Poetry as distinguished from the particular form in which it may be manifested.

The poets of the higher order are susceptible of a still further subdivision. There are those who project themselves out of their own particular being, and become by imagination one with that on which they meditate; and those who inform all they gaze on with their own individuality. Those, that is, who sympathize with all that is created; and those whose imagination makes all to sympathize with them. I need not say which of these two classes is the domain of the higher Poetry. Wherever egoism enters, whether it be into life or into art, it degrades and narrows; he through whom the universe speaks what God intended it to speak, is, as a poet, greater than he who through all the universe still only speaks out himself.

Now remark the different influence of these classes.

First, we have those whose imagination represents all nature as sympathizing with them; and just as through a coloured glass a landscape looks red, blue, or yellow, as the glass may be tinted, so does one feeling modify all others, and colour all things with its own hue. In some measure this is true of us all.

> "I may not hope from outward forms to win
> The passion and the life, whose fountains are within.
> O Lady! we receive but what we give,
> And in our life alone does nature live:
> Ours is her wedding garment, ours her shroud!" *

We all possess this tendency when the imagination has been intensified by one single passion, or narrowed by one absorbing pursuit. Let me give you a very homely illustration. I was once passing through the finest street in England on the outside of a mail coach. A young woman who sat near me, when we had reached the end of the street, suddenly exclaimed, "I never saw

* Coleridge—"Ode to Dejection."

so many narrow doors in all my life!" When the first surprise, produced by an exclamation so much in discord with my own thoughts, had subsided, I began to make inquiries, and discovered that her father was a builder. The builder's daughter had cast the hue of her daily associations over every thing. To her the buildings gray with the hoar of ages were as if they were not; historical interest, architectural beauty, solemn associations did not exist. To her there was nothing there but stones, graven by the stonemason's chisel, and doors, measurable by the rule of the carpenter. And in the same way do we all colour nature with our own pursuits. To a sportsman, a rich field is covert for game; to a farmer, the result of guano; to a geologist, indication of a certain character of subjacent rock.

It is very instructive to observe how superstition can thus summon all nature to be the minister of our human history, especially when it is rendered more imperious in its demands by pride. There is scarcely an ancient family which has not the tradition of preternatural appearances preceding the death or connected with the destinies of the chief members of the race. Shakspeare, as usual, gives us this. Lear's anguish sheds the hue of ingratitude over the heavens. To Timon, sun, and moon, and stars are tinctured with his misanthropy. To Macbeth, meditating murder, all nature is preternatural, sounds of simple instinct ominous, and all things conscious of his secret.

> "Now o'er the one half-world
> Nature seems dead, and wicked dreams abuse
> The curtain'd sleep; now witchcraft celebrates
> Pale Hecate's offerings; and withered murther,
> Alarum'd by his sentinel, the wolf,
> Whose howl's his watch, thus with his stealthy pace,
> With Tarquin's ravishing strides, towards his design
> Moves like a ghost. Thou sure and firm-set earth,
> Hear not my steps, which way they walk, for fear
> Thy very stones prate of my whereabout,
> And take the present horror from the time,
> Which now suits with it."

> "Come, sealing night,
> Scarf up the tender eye of pitiful day;
> And, with thy bloody and invisible hand,
> Cancel, and tear to pieces, that great bond
> Which keeps me pale! Light thickens; and the crow
> Makes wing to the rooky wood;
> Good things of day begin to droop and drowse;
> While night's black agents to their prey do rouse!"

Observe, again, how Casca's conscience, already half-burdened, distorts the simplest phenomena:—

> "Against the capitol I met a lion,
> Who glared upon me, and went surly by

Without annoying me; and there were drawn
Upon a heap a hundred ghastly women
Transformed with their fear; who swore they saw
Men all in fire walk up and down the streets.
And yesterday, the bird of night did sit
Even at noonday, upon the market place,
Hooting and shrieking."

Of all this apparent supernaturalism, Cicero gives the true account, in reply :—

"Indeed, it is a strange disposed time;
But men may construe things after their fashion,
Clean from the purpose of the things themselves."

And Calphurnia, with a presentiment of her husband's doom :—

"There is one within,
Besides the things that we have heard and seen,
Recounts most horrid sights seen by the watch.
A lioness hath whelped in the streets:
And graves have yawned and yielded up their dead:
Fierce, fiery warriors fight upon the clouds
In ranks and squadrons and right form of war,
Which drizzled blood upon the capitol:
The noise of battle hurtled in the air,
Horses do neigh, and dying men did groan:
And ghosts did shriek and squeal about the streets."

Mark, too, how, as I said, pride has its share in giving shape to this superstition. Cæsar replies, the valour of the conqueror defying omens, and the large heart of the man recognizing his subjection to the laws of a common humanity:

> "Yet Cæsar shall go forth: for these predictions
> Are to the world in general, as to Cæsar."

But Calphurnia, with that worship of high birth which is peculiar to the feminine nature, answers:—

> "When beggars die there are no comets seen:
> The heavens themselves blaze forth the death of princes."

So wonderful is that egoism of man which can thus overspread the heavens with its woes, and read in the planets only prophecies of himself! Now that which belongs to us all in some moods, is characteristic of some poets through all their nature, and pervades their work. The influence, therefore, of this class of Poetry, depends upon the *man*. The self which is thrown upon nature may be the lower or the higher self, and the influence will be correspondingly of the lower or the higher kind.

Among the former divisions of the egoistic class of first-rate poets, severe justice compels me with pain to place Lord Byron. Brought up under the baleful influences of Calvinism, which makes sovereign Will the measure of Right, instead of Right the cause and law of Will, a system which he all his life hated and believed—

fancying himself the mark of an inexorable decree, and bidding a terrible defiance to the unjust One who had fixed his doom—no wonder that, as in that strange phenomenon the spectre of the Brocken, the traveller sees a gigantic form cast upon the mists, which he discovers at last to be but his own shadow; so, the noble poet went through life haunted, turn which way he would, with the gigantic shadow of himself, which obscured the heavens and turned the light into thick darkness.

Foremost among those in whom a higher self informs all objects, stands Milton. We are compelled to place him with those in whom egoism is not wholly absorbed in nature. Shakspeare is a "voice." Read Shakspeare through, and, except from some of his sonnets, you could not guess who or what manner of man he was. But you could not read Milton long without discovering the man through the poet. His domestic miseries are reflected in his "Samson Agonistes." In his "Comus," that majestic psalm to Chastity, are blended the antique heroism of his Pagan studies, and the Christian sanctities of his rare manhood. His very angels reason upon Puritan questions; and it was the taunt of Pope, that in the Eternal lips themselves, redemption is a contrivance or scheme according to the systematic theology of a school divine. And yet the egoism with which all his Poetry is impregnated is the egoism of a glorious nature. If we were asked who in the eighteen Christian centuries stands before us as the highest approximation to what we conceive as Christian manhood, in which are rarely blended the opposites of purity and passion, gracefulness and strength, sanctity and manifold fitness for all the worldly duties of the man and the citizen, we should scarcely hesitate to answer —John Milton. The poet is overshadowed by the individual man: but the influence of the man is all for good.

Now compare with these the poets who see in Nature not themselves, but Nature; who are her voice, not she theirs. Of this class, likewise, there are two divisions: the first represented by Shakspeare, the second by Wordsworth.

Shakspeare is an universal poet, because he utters all that is in men; Wordsworth, because he speaks that which is in all men. There is much difference between these two statements.

The perfection of Shakspeare, like all the highest perfection, consists, not in the predominance of a single quality, or feeling, but in the just balance and perfect harmony of all. You cannot say whether the tragic element of our nature, or the comic, predominates; whether he has more sympathy with its broad laugh, or its secret sigh; with the contemplativeness of Hamlet, which lets the moment of action pass, or the promptitude of Hotspur; with the aristocratic pride of Coriolanus, which cannot deign to canvass the mob for votes, or the coarse wit and human instincts of the serving-men.

Wordsworth, on the contrary, gives to us humanity stripped of its peculiarities; the feelings which do not belong to this man or that, this or that age, but are the heritage of our common nature. "That," says he in a private letter, "which will distinguish my poems hereafter from those of other poets, is this: that while other poets laboured to exhibit that which distinguishes one man from another, especially the dramatic poets, I have made it my concern to exhibit that which is common to all men."

As a specimen of this, take that well-known poem:

"She was a phantom of delight,
When first she gleamed upon my sight;
A lovely apparition, sent
To be a moment's ornament;
Her eyes as stars of twilight fair;
Like twilight's, too, her dusky hair;
But all things else about her drawn
From May-time's brightest, loveliest dawn;

A dancing shape, an image gay,
To haunt, to startle, and waylay.

"I saw her upon nearer view,
A spirit, yet a woman too!
Her household motions light and free,
And steps of virgin liberty;
A countenance in which did meet
Sweet records, promises as sweet;
A creature not too bright or good
For human nature's daily food;
For transient sorrows, simple wiles,
Praise, blame, love, kisses, tears, and smiles.

"And now I see with eye serene
The very pulse of the machine;
A being breathing thoughtful breath,
A traveller between life and death;
The reason firm, the temperate will,
Endurance, foresight, strength, and skill;
A perfect woman, nobly planned,
To warn, to comfort, and command;
And yet a spirit still, and bright,
With something of an angel light."

You will observe that it is not a portrait like one of Shakspeare's, in which, gradually, a particular female character unfolds a personality which belongs to Miranda or to Juliet, and could not belong to Cleopatra or to Lady Macbeth; nor a description like Tennyson's, which, if true of Isabel or Lilian, must be false of Adeline or

Eleanore: nor, again, this or that woman, coloured in the false hues which passion or fancy have thrown on her for a time: but womanhood in its essence, and divested of its peculiarities of nation or century; such as her Creator meant her to be; such as every woman is potentially if not actually; such as she appears successively to the lover, the husband, and the friend, separating from such lover, husband, and friend, the accidents of an English, Spanish, or French temperament. And yet, remark that this womanhood, so painted, is not a mere thin, unsubstantial abstraction of the intellect; but a living, tangible image, appreciable by the senses, a single, total impression, "sensuous," as Milton says of Poetry: else it would not be Poetry, but a scientific definition. You have before you an ideal clothed in flesh and blood, without the limitations of any particular idiosyncrasy.

This is the sense in which poets like Wordsworth are universal poets and free from egoism; very different from the sense in which Shakspeare is universal.

Now to compare the various influences of these poets. And, first, to compare class with class. The poet in whom individuality predominates will have a more definite influence; he of whom universality is the characteristic, a more wide and lasting one. The influence of Cowper, Milton, or Byron, on individuals is distinct and appreciable; that of Homer and Shakspeare, almost imperceptible on single minds, is spread silently over ages, and determines the character of the world's literature and the world's feeling.

Comparing each class with itself, and taking first that which we have characterized as the more egoistic, the more popular will be almost always the less pure, because the passionate enthusiasm for what is great and good is shared by few, comparatively with the power of comprehending the might and force of what we commonly call the passions. Milton is placed with honour on our shelves. We read Byron through and through.

Next, of the poets of nature, Shakspeare, and the very few who can be ranked with him, will be more popular than such as Wordsworth; not because he is greater, though he is, of course, immeasurably, but because his greatness, like that of nature's self, is broken into fragments, and all can find in him something corresponding with their humour. Only a few, like Herschel and Humboldt, can comprehend with something like adequateness the Cosmos, or Order of the Universe; there is no one who cannot read a page of it. And so, very few of those who talk of

Shakspeare's greatness, know *how* great he is; but all can mark with pencil dashes certain lines and detached acts; and if you examined the copy so dashed and marked, you would probably discover what in Shakspeare bears, or was supposed to bear, reference to the reader's own character, or more properly, illustrated his or her private prejudices, peculiarities, and personal history; but, unless a hand as free from egoism as Shakspeare's own had drawn the lines of approval, you would gain from the book of extracts made up of all such passages, not the nature of Man, but the idiosyncrasy of a man. Tell us, therefore, that a man's favourite poet is such as Wordsworth, and we know something about his character; but tell us that he delights in Shakspeare, and we know as yet no more of him than if it had been said that life has joys for him. He may be a Marlborough, or he may be a clown.

Permit me to offer you two pieces of advice, resulting from what has been said.

First, Cultivate universality of taste. There is no surer mark of a half-educated mind than the incapacity of admiring various forms of excellence. Men who cannot praise Dryden without dispraising Coleridge; nor feel the stern, earthly truthfulness of Crabbe without disparaging the wild, ethereal, impalpable music of Shelley: nor exalt Spenser except by sneering at Tennyson, are precisely the persons to whom it should in consistency seem strange that in God's world there is a place for the eagle and the wren, a separate grace to the swan and the humming-bird, their own fragrance to the cedar and the violet. Enlarge your tastes, that you may enlarge your hearts as well as your pleasures; feel all that is beautiful—love all that is good. The first maxim in religion and in art is—sever yourself from all sectarianism; pledge yourself to no school; cut your life adrift from all party; be a slave to no maxims; stand forth, unfettered and free, servant only to the truth. And if you say, "But this will force each of us to stand alone;" I reply—Yes, grandly alone! untrammelled by the prejudices of any, and free to admire the beauty, and love the goodness of them all.

Secondly, of the writers whom we called egoistic, in whom, that is, the man predominates over the poet, choose such only as are the unfeigned servants of goodness—I do not mean *goodliness*—to be your special favourites. In early life it is, I believe, from this class solely that our favourites are selected; and a man's character and mind are moulded for good or evil far more by the forms of imagination which surround his childhood than by any subsequent scientific training.

We can recollect how a couplet from the frontispiece of a hymn-book struck deeper roots into our being, and has borne more manifest fruits, than all the formal training we ever got. Or we can trace, as unerringly as an Indian on the trail, the several influences of each poet through our lives: the sense of unjust destiny which was created by Byron; the taint of Moore's voluptuousness; the hearty, healthful life of Scott; the calming power of Wordsworth; the masculine vigour of Dryden. For it is only in after years that the real taste for the very highest Poetry is acquired. Life, and experience, as well as mental cultivation, are indispensable. In earlier life the influence of the man is mightier than that of the poet. Therefore, let every young man especially guard his heart and imagination against the mastery of those writers who sap his vigour and taint his purity.

We proceed to name a few of the modes in which Poetry does actually influence men:

First. In the way of giving relief to feeling. It is a law of our nature that strong feeling, unexpressed either in words or action, becomes morbid. You need not dread the passionate man, whose wrath vents itself in words; dread the man who grows pale, and suppresses the language of his resentment. There is something in him yet to come out. This is the secret of England's freedom from revolution and conspiracies; she has free discussion. Wrongs do not smoulder silently, to burst forth unexpectedly. Every grievance may have a hearing, and not being pent up, spends itself before it is dangerous.

> "The land where, girt by friend or foe,
> A man may speak the thing he will." *

Now, there are feelings which, unuttered, would make a man dangerous—or morbid—or mad;—utterance relieves, and, weakening the *feeling*, makes the *man* strong.

> "To me alone there came a thought of grief:
> A timely utterance gave that thought relief,
> And I again am strong."

For such feelings the poets find us suitable expression. In an artificial state of society, perhaps some young, warlike spirit pines for a more dangerous life than our quiet days give. Well, he reads Scott's border raids, or "Scots wha hae wi' Wallace bled," or "Hohen Linden," and the vivid forms of imagination receive, as it were, his superfluous energies, and the chafing subsides in unreal battle-fields: or some diseased germ of misanthropy is enlarging in his heart—secret discontent with life; disagreement with the world;

* Tennyson.

conflict between his nature and civil regulations; let him read Byron—a dangerous cure—but in the end a certain one. Byron has said all that can be said upon the subject. What more can be added? There is no restless feeling left behind of something unsaid. Exhaustion follows—then health. For it is a mistake to think that Poetry is only good to nurse feeling. It is good for enabling us to *get rid* of feeling for which there is no available field of action. It is the safety-valve to the heart.

It has, besides, an elevating influence. It breaks the monotonous flatness of existence by excitement. Its very essence is that it exalts us, and puts us in a higher mood than that in which we live habitually. And this is peculiarly true of modern Poetry. A great critic* has said that the distinction between ancient and modern Poetry is, that the characteristic of the former is satisfaction, that of the latter aspiration. To the ancients this time-world was all. To round it with completeness, and hold all powers in harmonious balance, was their whole aim. Whereas, Christianity has dwarfed this life in comparison with the thought of an endless existence which it has revealed. To them the thought of death only came as a stimulus to increased enjoyment of

* Schlegel.

that which must soon pass. To us that thought comes moderating and calming all pleasure. And hence the sad, dark character of Christian, especially northern Poetry; as the utterance of a heart which is conscious of eternal discord rather than of perfection of powers; and through it all there vibrates an undertone of melancholy, adding even to mirth a peculiar pathos. Is it not better that it should be so? Does not such Poetry therefore more peculiarly belong to Working Men, whose life is desire, not enjoyment; aspiration, not contentment?

Whoever will go into any Gothic cathedral in the evening, knowing nothing of the connoisseurship of architecture, and watch the effect produced on his mind by the lines which wander away, bewildering the eye with the feeling of endlessness, and losing themselves in the dark distances, and will then compare the total impression with that produced by the voluptuous, earthly beauty of a temple like the Madeleine in Paris, will understand, without the help of any scientific jargon, the difference between the ancient idea of satisfaction and the modern one of aspiration.

But when we say Poetry elevates, let it not be understood of the improvement of physical comforts. Poetry will not place a man in better circumstances; but it may raise him above his circumstances, and fortify him with inward independence; as Lovelace, the cavalier poet, has very gracefully expressed, in lines written in confinement:—

"Stone walls do not a prison make,
Nor iron bars a cage;
Minds innocent and quiet take
That for a hermitage.

"If I have freedom in my love,
And in my soul am free,
Angels alone, that soar above,
Enjoy such liberty."

And yet, as there are some persons who cannot conceive of human elevation except as connected with circumstantial condition, I must tell you an anecdote to satisfy even them. A lady, with whose friendship I am honoured, was travelling last summer in the Lake district of Cumberland and Westmoreland. Being interested in education, she visited many of the National Schools in that country. For the most part the result was uninteresting enough. The heavy looks and stolid intellects, which characterize our English agricultural population, disappointed her. But in one place there was a striking difference. The children were sprightly, alert, and answered with intelligence all the questions proposed; traced rivers from their sources to the sea, explaining why the towns along their course were of such and such a character, and how the soil had modified the habits and lives of the inhabitants—with much of similar information. The schoolmaster had been educated at one of our great training seminaries. He was invited by the tourist to spend an hour at the hotel; and when, after a long conversation, she expressed her surprise that one so highly educated should bury himself in a retired, unknown spot, with small stipend, teaching only a few rustics, he replied, after some hesitation—"Why, Madam, when this situation was first offered me, I was on the point of marriage; and I calculated that it would be worth more to me to live on a small salary, with domestic peace, in the midst of this beautiful scenery, than on a much larger sum in a less glorious spot."

Now, there are people who can only estimate the worth of a thing by what it will bring. What is the *use* of Poetry? Well, perhaps they may answer that question for themselves, if I have shown that refined taste may be an equivalent for half an income, and a sense of what is beautiful in God's world may make a poor man

"passing rich with forty pounds a-year."

The tendency, again, of Poetry is to unite

men together. And this both indirectly and directly.

It has been already said that the highest Poetry is that which represents the most universal feeling, not the most rare. It is in this sense that Milton's definition makes Poetry "simple;" that is, it deals with the feelings which we have in common, as men, and not with those which we possess as a particular sort or class of men; with the natural rather than the trained, artificial, or acquired feelings; just as the botanist is simple in contrast with the horticulturist. The one seeks what is natural; and to him nothing in nature is a weed. The other seeks rarities and hotbed monstrosities.

The Germans say that the world has produced only three poets of firstrate genius:—Homer, Shakspeare, and Goethe. This, I suppose, is an exaggeration; nevertheless, it is true that the highest poets have been, like them, not a class or caste, but of humanity. Take, almost at a venture, the first familiar names that present themselves.

Milton, by all the associations of education and refined tastes, belonged to the royalists and the Church; but he threw himself, in spite of the vulgarities which repelled him personally from its worship, and left him at last without visible worship, on the side of the conventicle, because in the days of the Stuarts the cause of the conventicle was the cause of liberty and truth.

Dante was a Romanist; but no slave was he of popery. His world-wide conception represents the heathens and the Christians of all ages as the subjects of one moral government, responsible to the laws impressed upon humanity rather than those written by the Church; and his severe justice does not scruple to consign a long list of bishops and popes to the eternal penalty of crimes.

Or, again, Byron and Shelley—aristocrats both by birth, yet no minions of a caste, nor champions of hereditary privilege—they were men; and their power lay in this, that they were the champions of human rights, as well as utterers of the passion that is in men. So far as they are great, they are universal; so far as they are small or bad, they are narrow and egotistical. And as time rolls on, that which is of self, limited and evil, will become obsolete, and wither, as the mortal warp and woof shrivelled on the arm of Halbert Glendinning, when he plunged it into the sacred flame to grasp the Volume of Truth at the bidding of the White Lady of Avenel; and that of their works which will remain unconsumed will be the living flesh of the humanity that never dies—so much as is true to universal nature and to fact.

It is thus that the poets universalize and unite. "One touch of nature makes the whole world kin." And, hence, Poetry has been silently doing a work for the poorer classes when they were not aware of it; for even that Poetry which does not interest them, may be opening the hearts of the richer classes towards them. Did Burns teach the nobles no sympathy with the cares, and the loves, and the trials of the cotter's life? And when poor Hood wrote the "Song of the Shirt," so touchingly expressive of the sorrows of an unknown class, the over-worked needlewoman, and all England, thrilled to the appeal:

> "O men, with sisters dear!
> O men, with mothers and wives!
> It is not linen you're wearing out,
> But human creatures' lives—"

and when, in consequence, plan after plan was tried, and investigations instituted, and a kindlier interest evoked to ameliorate their condition, tell us—Had Poetry done nothing for the Working Classes?

But it has a more direct influence than this in the way of uniting. Chiefly from that power with which the poetic nature is peculiarly gifted of discovering what Shakspeare calls the "soul of goodness in things evil." Every great poet is a "double natured man;" with the feminine and manly powers in harmonious union; having the tact, and the sympathy, and the intuition, and the tenderness of woman, with the breadth and massiveness of the manly intellect, besides the calm justice which is almost exclusively masculine. For this reason a poet, seeing into the life of things, is not one-sided; can see the truth which lies at the root of error; can blame evil without hysterically raving against every doer of it; distinguishes between frailty and villany; judges leniently, because by sympathy he can look upon faults as they appear to those who committed them; judges justly, because, so far as he is an artist, he can regard the feeling with which he sympathizes from without; in a double way—realizing it, but not surrendered to it.

I must quote two passages explanatory of the world of meaning contained in those few words of Shakspeare: the "soul of goodness in things evil."

Wordsworth means the same when he says:—

> "'Tis Nature's law
> That none, the meanest of created things,
> Of forms created the most vile and brute,
> The dullest or most noxious, should exist,
> Divorced from good—a spirit and pulse of good,
> A life and soul, to every mode of being
> Inseparably linked. Then be assured
> That least of all can aught—that ever owned

The heaven-regarding eye and front sublime
Which man is born to, sink, howe'ver depressed,
So low as to be scorned without a sin;
Without offence to God cast out of view."

And again :—

" He who feels contempt
For any living thing, hath faculties
That he hath never used: and Thought with him
Is in its infancy."

One of the best illustrations I can remember of this prerogative of the poet to fasten the attention on what is human and loveable, rather than on what is evil, is Hood's "Bridge of Sighs." This little poem is suggested by the sight of a poor suicide, who has cast herself from one of the London bridges. Prudery, male or female, would turn from such a spectacle with disgust; the disciple of some school of cold divinity would see in it only a text for a discourse on hell. The poet discerns something in it of a deeper mystery, not so flippantly to be solved. He bids you

" Touch her not scornfully,
Think of her mournfully,
Gently and humanly;
Not of the stains of her;
All that remains of her
Now is pure womanly.
Make no deep scrutiny
Into her mutiny

Rash and undutiful;
Past all dishonour,
Death has left on her
Only the beautiful."

And observe how, with exquisite truthfulness, he fixes your attention, not upon that in which the poor outcast differs from you, but on that in which her sisterhood to the human family consisted—and, for aught *you* may dare to say, still consists—

"Wonderment guesses
Where was her home?
Who was her father?
Who was her mother?
Had she a sister?
Had she a brother?
Or was there a nearer one
Still, and a dearer one
Yet, than all other?"

And mark how—without any feeble sentimentalism, without once confusing the boundaries of right and wrong, without hinting a suspicion that vice is not vice, and wrong not wrong—he simply reminds you that judgment does not belong to you, a fellow-creature and a sinner; and bids you place her in the attitude in which alone *you* have a right to regard her now—

"Cross her hands humbly,
As if praying dumbly,

Over her breast;
Owning her weakness,
Her evil behaviour,
And leaving in meekness
Her sins to her Saviour."

I should not like to be the woman who could read that poem without something more than sentimental tears, an enlarged humanity, and a deeper justice; nor should I like to be the man who could rise from the perusal of it without a mighty throb added to the conviction that libertinism is a thing of damnable and selfish cowardice.

Again, Poetry discovers good in men who differ from us, and so teaches us that we are one with them. For the poet belongs to the world rather than to his party; speaks his party's feelings, which are human; not their watchwords and formulas, which, being forms of the intellect, are transitory, often false, always limited. Thus, Romanism and Puritanism, and their modern feeble descendants, as dogmatic systems, are forbidding enough. But listen to Dante, and you will feel that purgatory, false as a dogma, is true as the symbolism of an everlasting fact of the human soul. Hear Milton sing, and the *heart* of Puritanism is recognized as a noble and a manly thing. And, however repelled you may be by the false metaphysics, the pretensions to infallible interpretations, the cant phrases, and the impotent intolerance which characterize the dwarfed and dwindled Puritanism of our own days, out of which all pith and manhood appear to have departed, who does not feel disposed to be tender to it for Cowper's gentle sake? However out of date the effort of the Tractarian may seem to you, to reproduce the piety of the past through the forms of the past, instead of striving, like a true prophet, to interpret the aspirations of the present in forms which shall truly represent and foster them, what man is there to whose heart Keble has not shown that in Tractarianism, too, there is a "soul of goodness," a life and a meaning which mere negations cannot destroy?

Lastly, I name the refining influence of Poetry. We shall confine our proofs to that which it has already done in making men and life less savage, carnal, and mercenary; and this especially in the three departments which were the peculiar sphere of the Poetry which is called romantic. Beneath its influence, passion became love; selfishness, honour; and war, chivalry.

The first of these, as a high sentiment, can only be said to have come into existence with the Christianity of the Middle Ages. All who are familiar with the Greek and Roman Poetry, know that the sentiment which now bears the name, was unknown to the ancients. It became what it is when passion had been hallowed by imagination. Then, and not till then, it became loyalty to female worth, consecrated by religion. For the sacred thought of a Virgin Mother spread its sanctity over the whole idea of the sex. Christianity had given to the world a new object for its imagination; and the idolatry into which it passed in the Church of Rome, was but the inevitable result of the effort of rude minds struggling to express in form the new idea of a divine sacredness belonging to feminine qualities of meekness and purity, which the ages before had overlooked. That this influence of the religious element of the imagination on the earthlier feeling is not fanciful but historical, might be shown in the single case of Ignatius Loyola, on whose ardent temperament the influences of his age worked strongly. Hence it was that there seemed nothing profane when the chivalrous gallantry of the soldier transformed itself by, to him, a most natural transition, into a loyal dedication of all his powers to One who was "not a countess, nor a duchess, but much greater." But only think how he must have shrunk from this transference of homage, as blasphemous, if his former earthlier feelings had not been elevated by a religious imagination; if, in short, his affections had been like those of the Greeks and Romans!

And while on the subject of the influence of all the higher feelings in elevating passion into that which is unselfish and pure, and even sublime, I will remind you of those glorious lines of Lovelace in reply to a reproach on account of absence caused by duty:

> "Yet this inconstancy is such
> As you, too, shall adore;
> I could not love thee, dear, so much,
> Loved I not honour more."

Under the influence of imagination, selfishness became honour. Doubtless, the law of honour is only half Christian. Yet it did this: it proclaimed the invisible truth above the visible comfort. It consecrated certain acts as right, uncalculatingly, and independently of consequences. It did not say—it will be *better* for you in the end if you do honourably. It said—you *must* do honourably, though it be not better for you to do it, but worse, and deathful. It was not religion; but it was better than the popular, merely prudential, mercenary religion, which says, "Honesty is the best policy; godliness is gain; do right and you will not lose by it." Honour said, Perhaps you *will* lose—all—life; lose then, like a man; for there is something higher than life, dearer than even *your* eternal gain. It was not purely religious; for it retained the selfish element. But it was a more refined selfishness which permitted a man to take another's life in defence of his honour, than that which requires him to do it in defence of his purse.

Finally, through poetic imagination war became chivalry. The practice of arms ceased to be "a conflict of kites and crows;" it was guarded by a refined courtesy from every rude and ungenerous abuse of superior strength.

Upon this point there is much sophistry prevalent; therefore it is worth while to see how the matter really stands. A truly great man—the American Channing—has said, I remember, somewhere in his works, that if armies were dressed in a hangman's or a butcher's garb, the false glare of military enthusiasm would be destroyed, and war would be seen in its true aspect as butchery.

It is wonderful how the generous enthusiasm of Dr. Channing has led him into such a sophism. Take away honour, and imagination, and Poetry from war, and it becomes carnage. Doubtless. And take away public spirit and invisible principles from resistance to a tax, and Hampden becomes a noisy demagogue. Take away the grandeur of his cause, and Washington is a rebel, instead of the purest of patriots. Take away imagination from love, and what remains? Let a people treat with scorn the defenders of its liberties, and invest them with the symbols of degradation, and it will soon have no one to defend it. This is but a truism.

But it is a falsity if it implies that the mere change of symbolic dress, unless the dress truly represented a previous change of public feeling, would reverse the feeling with which the profession of arms is regarded. So long as people found it impossible to confound the warrior with the hangman, all that a change of garb could do would be to invest the sign with new dignity. Things mean become noble by association; the Thistle—the Leek—the Broom of the Plantagenets—the Garter—and the Death's Head and Cross Bones on the front of the Black Brunswickers, typical of the stern resolve to avenge their Chief—methinks those symbols did not exactly change the soldier into a sexton!

But the truth is that here, as elsewhere, Poetry has reached the truth, while science and common-sense have missed it. It has distinguished—as, in spite of all mercenary and feeble sophistry, men ever will distinguish—war from mere bloodshed. It has discerned the higher feelings which lie beneath its revolting features. Carnage is terrible. The conversion of producers into destroyers is a calamity. Death, and insults to woman worse than death—and human features obliterated beneath the hoof of the war-horse—and reeking hospitals, and ruined commerce, and violated homes, and broken hearts—they are all awful. But there is something worse than death. Cowardice is worse. And the decay of enthusiasm and manliness is worse. And it is worse than death, aye, worse than a hundred thousand deaths, when a people has gravitated down into the creed that the "wealth of nations" consists, not in generous hearts—"Fire in each breast, and freedom on each brow"—in national virtues, and primitive simplicity, and heroic endurance, and preference of duty to life;—not in MEN, but in silk, and cotton, and something that they call "capital." Peace is blessed. Peace, arising out of charity. But peace, springing out of the calculations of selfishness, is not blessed. If the price to be paid for peace is this, that wealth accumulate and men decay, better far that every street in every town of our once noble country should run blood!

Through the physical horrors of warfare, Poetry discerned the redeeming nobleness. For in truth, when war is not prolonged, the kindling of all the higher passions prevents the access of the baser ones. A nation split and severed by mean religious and political dissensions, suddenly feels its unity, and men's hearts beat together, at the mere possibility of invasion. And even woman, as the author of the "History of the Peninsular War" has well remarked, sufferer as she is by war, yet gains; in the more chivalrous respect paid to her, in the elevation of the feelings excited towards her, in the attitude of protection assumed by men, and in the high calls to duty which arouse her from the frivolousness and feebleness into which her existence is apt to sink.

I will illustrate this by one more anecdote from the same campaign to which allusion has been already made — Sir Charles Napier's campaign against the robber tribes of Upper Scinde.

A detachment of troops was marching along a valley, the cliffs overhanging which were crested by the enemy. A sergeant, with eleven men, chanced to become separated from the rest by taking the wrong side of a ravine, which they expected soon to terminate, but which suddenly deepened into an impassable chasm. The officer in command signalled to the party an order to return. They mistook the signal for a command to charge; the brave fellows answered with a cheer, and charged. At the summit of the steep mountain was a triangular platform, defended by a breastwork, behind which were seventy of the foe. On they went, charging up one of those fearful paths, eleven against seventy. The contest could not long be doubtful with such odds. One after another they fell; six upon the spot, the remainder hurled backwards; but not until they had slain nearly twice their own number.

There is a custom, we are told, amongst the hillsmen, that when a great chieftain of their own falls in battle, his wrist is bound with a thread either of red or green, the red denoting the highest rank. According to custom, they stripped the dead, and threw their bodies over the precipice. When their comrades came, they found their corpses stark and gashed; but round both wrists of every British hero was twined the red thread! *

I think you will perceive how Poetry, expressing in this rude symbolism unutterable admiration of heroic daring, had given another aspect to war than that of butchery; and you will understand how, with such a foe, and such a general as the English commander, who more than once refused battle because the wives and children of the enemy were in the hostile camp, and he feared for their lives, carnage changed its character, and

* "History of the Administration of Scinde," by Lieut. Gen. Sir William Napier.

became chivalry; and how it was that the British troops learned to treat their captive women with respect; and the chieftains of the Cutchee hills offered their swords and services with enthusiasm to their conqueror; and the wild hill-tribes, transplanted to the plains, became as persevering in agriculture as they had been before in war.

And now to conclude. They tell us that scenes such as this may be called for in this our England. I do not pretend to judge. We only know that a military nation is at our doors with 450,000 gallant soldiers under arms, every man burning to wipe out the memory of past defeats, with one at their head the prestige of whose name recalls an era of unparalleled brilliancy, many of them trained in a school of warfare where the razzias of Africa have not taught either scrupulosity or mercifulness. We know that a chieftain who is to rule France with any hope of imperial influence, can best secure enthusiasm by giving victory to her armies; and that French generals have already specified the way in which—I quote the words of Paixham—a lesson might be taught to England which she should not soon forget.

No one who loves his country,—no one who knows what is meant by the *sack of a town*, especially by French soldiers,—can contemplate the possibility of such an event, without a fervent hope that that day may never come. Nor does it become us to boast; the enthusiasm of the platform is easy, and costs little; and we may be called upon, before very long, to show by something more than words, whether there be steel in our hearts and hands, or not.

But thus much I will dare to say. If a foreign foot be planted on our sacred soil—if the ring of the rifle of the Chasseurs de Vincennes be heard upon these shores, terrible as the first reverses might be, when discipline could be met only by raw enthusiasm—thanks to gentlemen who have taught us the sublime mysteries of "capital" in lieu of the old English superstitions of Honour and Religion—they may yet chance to learn that British Chivalry did not breathe her last at Moodkee or Ferozeshah, or Sobraon, or Goojerat, or Meeanee, or Hyderabad. They may yet be taught that there is something beyond the raw hysterics of a transient excitement in the spirit of self-sacrifice which we have learned from our Master's cross. They may yet discover that amongst the artisans, and peasants, and working men of England, there are a thousand thousand worthy to be brothers of those heroic eleven who sleep beneath the rocks of Trukkee, with the red thread of Honour round their wrists.

LECTURE ON WORDSWORTH.

Lecture on Wordsworth, delivered to the Members of the Brighton Athenæum, on February 10*th*, 1853.

In order to treat fully the subject which I have to bring before you this evening, I believe there are three points to which I ought principally to direct your attention. The first is, the qualifications necessary for appreciating poetry in general, and for appreciating the poetry of Wordsworth in particular. The second is the character and life of Wordsworth, so far as they bear upon his poetry, and so far as they may have been supposed to have formed or modified his peculiar poetical theories and principles. The third point is, the theories and poetical principles of Wordsworth, and how far they are true, how far they have been exaggerated, and how far Wordsworth has himself worked out the principles he has laid down.

Now, it will be plain that the last of these is the most important point of all; it is, in fact, *the* subject of our consideration; but so many preliminary subjects have presented themselves which must be gone into before we enter upon this, that I have found it necessary to reserve this third topic for a succeeding lecture,* confining myself on the present occasion merely to the two first points that I have already named.

I have undertaken to lecture this evening upon Wordsworth. To some persons this will appear presumption; to others, it will appear superfluous. To all the admirers of Wordsworth's genius, it will appear presumption. To these I simply reply, I know well the difficulty of the subject, I know how impossible it is to treat it adequately; I am aware that presumption is implied in the thought, that before it is possible to criticize a man one must sympathize with him, and that to sympathize with a man implies that there is, to a certain extent, a power of breathing the same atmosphere. Nevertheless, I reply that it is with me, at least, a work and labour of love; nor can I believe, that any one who has for years studied Wordsworth and loved him, and year by year felt his appreciation and comprehension of Wordsworth grow, and has during all those years endeavoured to make Wordsworth's principles the guiding principles of his own inner life

* This lecture was never delivered, owing to Mr. Robertson's ill-health.

—I cannot believe that such a man can have nothing to say which it can be desirable should be heard by his fellow men.

There is another class, however, to whom such a subject will seem superfluous; for the general opinion about Wordsworth is exceedingly superficial. To the mass of the public all that is known of Wordsworth is a conception something like this: They have heard of an old man who lived somewhere in the Lake districts, who raved considerably of Lake scenery, who wrote a large number of small poems, all of them innocent, many of them puerile and much laughed at, at the time they appeared, by clever men; that they were lashed in the reviews, and annihilated by Lord Byron, as, for instance, in those well-known lines—

> "A drowsy, frowsy poem, called the Excursion,
> Writ in a manner which is my aversion;"

and that he was guilty of a vast mass of other verses, all exceedingly innocent, and at the same time exceedingly dull and heavy. It is this class of persons whom I ask on the present occasion to listen quietly to the first subject I have to bring before them—the qualifications necessary for appreciating poetry in general and Wordsworth's poetry in particular.

Now, the first qualification I shall speak of as

necessary for appreciating poetry is unworldliness. Let us understand the term employed. By worldliness, I mean entanglement in the temporal and visible. It is the spirit of worldliness which makes a man love show, splendour, rank, title, and sensual enjoyments; and occupies his attention, chiefly or entirely, with conversations respecting merely passing events, and passing acquaintances. I know not that I could give a more distinct idea of what I mean by unworldliness, than by relating an anecdote of a boy of rare genius, inheriting genius from both parents, who, when he began the study of mathematics, was impressed with so strange and solemn a sense of awe, that never before, he said, had he been able to comprehend the existence of the Eternal. It is not difficult to understand what the boy meant. Mathematics contain truths entirely independent of Time and Space; they tell of relations which have no connection, necessarily, with weight or quality; they deal with the eternal principles and laws of the mind; and it is certain, that these laws are more real and eternal than any thing which can be seen or felt. This is what I mean by unworldliness: I am not speaking of it as a theologian, or as a religionist, but I am speaking of unworldliness in that sense, of which it is true of all science and high art, as well as of Nature.

For all high art is essentially unworldliness, and the highest artists have been unworldly in aim, and unworldly in life.

Let us compare the life of Benvenuto Cellini. I name him, because there has been given recently to the public a life of him in a popular form. Let us compare his life with the life of Raphael, or Michael Angelo, or Beethoven, or Canova. You will be struck with this difference, that in Benvenuto Cellini there was an entire absence of any thing like aspiration beyond the Visible and the Seen; but in the life of the others there was the strong and perpetual conviction that the things seen were the things unreal, and that the things unseen were the things real; there was the perpetual desire to realize in a visible form, that beauty which the eye had not seen nor the ear heard, nor which it had ever entered into the heart of man to conceive. I will here quote one single passage in illustration of this; it is a translation by Wordsworth himself, from one of the sonnets of Michael Angelo: it is simply an illustration of what I have said:—

"Heaven-born, the soul a heavenward course must hold;
Beyond the visible world she soars to seek
(For what delights the sense is false and weak)
Ideal form, the universal mould.
The wise man, I affirm, can find no rest

In that which perishes; nor will he lend
His heart to aught which doth on time depend."

This is a view of high art: and in this respect poetry, like high art, and like religion, introduces its votaries into a world of which the senses take no cognizance; therefore I now maintain that until a man's eyes have been clarified by that power which enables him to look beyond the visible; until—

"He from thick films shall purge the visual ray,
And on the sightless eyeball pour the day,"

poetry—high poetry, like Wordsworth's—is simply and merely unintelligible.

I will give two or three illustrations of the way in which Wordsworth himself looked on this subject. The first is in reference to the power which there is in splendour and in riches to unfit the mind for the contemplation of invisible and spiritual truths. The sonnet I am about to read was written in September, 1802, the period during which the chief part of the poems I shall read this evening were written. I believe it was written to Coleridge.

"Oh! friend, I know not which way I must look
For comfort, being, as I am, opprest
To think that now our life is only drest
For show; mean handy-work of craftsman, cook,

Or groom!—We must run glittering like a brook
In the open sunshine, or we are unblest:
The wealthiest man among us is the best:
No grandeur now in nature or in book
Delights us."

The connection of these two things is what I wish to fasten your attention upon—

"The wealthiest man among us is the best,"

that being the spirit of society, then—

"No grandeur now in nature or in book
Delights us."

The second illustration is in reference to what is called scandal or gossip. According to Wordsworth, this is the highest manifestation of a worldly spirit. What is it but conversations respecting passing events or passing acquaintances, unappreciated and unelevated by high principle? Wordsworth has written four sonnets, worthy of deep study, on this subject. After stating the matter in the first of these, in the second he supposes a possible defence against this habit of general conversation respecting others, derisively.

"'Yet life,' you say, 'is life; we have seen and see
And with a lively pleasure we describe;
And fits of sprightly malice do but bribe
The languid mind into activity.
Sound sense, and love itself, and mirth and glee,
Are fostered by the comment and the gibe.'"

Then comes Wordsworth's comment:—

"Even be it so; yet still among your tribe,
Our daily world's true worldings, rank not me!
Children are blest and powerful; their world lies
More justly balanced; partly at their feet
And part far from them: sweetest melodies
Are those that are by distance made more sweet.
Whose mind is but the mind of his own eyes,
He is a slave; the meanest we can meet!"

To understand this, you must carry in your recollection what Wordsworth's views of childhood and infancy are, as given in the sublime "Ode to Immortality." A child, according to Wordsworth, is a being haunted for ever by eternal mind. He tells us that "Heaven lies about us in our infancy"—that the child moves perpetually in two worlds: the world that is seen right before him, and that terminated in another world—a world invisible, the glory of which is as from a palace—"That imperial palace whence he came;" and that high philosophy and poetry are nothing but this coming back to the simple state of childhood, in which we see not merely the thing before us, but the thing before us transfigured and irradiated by the perception of that higher life:—

"Children are blest and powerful; their world lies
More justly balanced; partly at their feet,
And part afar from them."

Then Wordsworth goes on to show how poetry supplies the place which scandal and gossip had occupied.

> "Dreams, books, are each a world; and books, we know,
> Are a substantial world, both pure and good:
> Round these, with tendrils strong as flesh and blood,
> Our pastime and our happiness will grow.
> There find I personal themes, a plenteous store,
> Matter wherein right voluble I am,
> To which I listen with a ready ear;
> Two shall be named, preëminently dear,—
> The gentle lady married to the Moor;
> And heavenly Una with her milk-white lamb."

In other words, scandal is nothing more than inverted love of humanity. An absolute necessity, Wordsworth tells us, exists within us for personal themes of conversation that have reference to human beings, and not to abstract principles; but when that necessity is gratified upon the concerns and occupations of those immediately around us, which necessarily become mixed with envy and evil feelings, then that necessity is inverted and perverted. So the place of detraction or scandal is by the poet occupied in personal themes; as, for example, when a man has made the object of his household thoughts such characters as Desdemona and Spenser's Una, then he has something which may carry his mind to high and true principles, beyond the present. Then Wordsworth goes on to say,—

"Nor can I not believe but that hereby
Great gains are mine; for thus I live remote
From evil speaking; rancour, never sought,
Comes to me not, malignant truth, nor lie.
Hence have I genial seasons, hence have I
Smooth passions, smooth discourse, and joyous thought:
And thus, from day to day my little boat
Rocks in its harbour, lodging peaceably.
Blessings be with them—and eternal praise,
Who gave us nobler loves, and nobler cares—
The Poets, who on earth have made us heirs
Of truth and pure delight by heavenly lays."

I shall now read you a passage from a letter written by Wordsworth to Lady Beaumont, in which he answers the objection that his poems were not popular, and explains the reason why in one sense his poetry never could be popular with the world of fashion.

"It is impossible that any expectations can be lower than mine concerning the immediate effect of this little work upon what is called the public. I do not here take into consideration the envy and malevolence, and all the bad passions, which always stand in the way of a work of any merit from a living poet; but merely think of the pure, absolute, honest ignorance in which all worldlings of every rank and situation must be enveloped, with respect to the thoughts, feelings, and images, on which the life of my poems depends. The things which I have taken, whether from within or without—what have they to do with routs, dinners, morning calls, hurry from door to door, from street to street, on foot or in carriage; with Mr. Pitt or Mr. Fox, Mr. Paul or Sir Francis Burdett, the Westminster election or the borough of Honiton? In a word—for I cannot stop to make my way through the hurry of images that present themselves to me—what have they to do with endless talking about things nobody cares anything for, except as far as their own vanity is concerned, and this with persons they care nothing for, but as their vanity or *selfishness* is concerned? What have they to do (to say all at once) with a life without love? In such a life there can be no thought; for we have no thoughts (save thoughts of pain,) but as far as we have love and admiration.

"It is an awful truth that there neither is, nor can be, any genuine enjoyment of poetry among nineteen out of twenty of those persons who live, or wish to live, in the broad light of the world—among those who either are, or are striving to make themselves, people of *consideration* in society. This is a truth, and an awful one; because to be incapable of a feeling of poetry, in my sense of the word, is to be without love of human nature and reverence for God.

"Upon this I shall insist elsewhere; at present, let me confine myself to my object, which is to make you, my dear friend, as easy-hearted as myself with respect to these poems. Trouble not yourself upon their present reception: of what moment is that, compared with what I trust is their destiny?—to console the afflicted; to add sunshine to daylight, by making the happy happier; to teach the young and the gracious of every age to see, to think, and feel, and therefore to become more actively and securely virtuous—this is their office, which I trust they will faithfully perform, long after we (that is, all that is mortal of us) are mouldered in our graves."

And then, after some striking criticisms and analyses of his own poetry, he continues:—

"Be assured that the decision of these persons has nothing to do with the question; they are altogether incompetent judges. These people, in the senseless hurry of their idle lives, do not *read* books; they merely snatch a glance at them that they may talk about them. And even if this were not so, never forget what, I believe, was observed to you by Coleridge—that every great and original writer, in proportion as he is great or original, must himself create the taste by which he is to be relished; he must teach the art by which he is to be seen; this, in a certain degree, even to all persons, however wise and pure may be their lives, and however unvitiated their taste. But for those who dip into books in order to give an opinion of them, or talk about them to take up an opinion—for this multitude of unhappy, and misguided, and misguiding beings, an entire regeneration must be produced; and if this be possible, it must be a work *of time.* To conclude, my ears are stone-dead to this idle buzz, and my flesh as insensible as iron to these petty stings; and, after what I have said, I am sure yours will be the same. I doubt not that you will share with me an invincible confidence that my writings (and among them these little poems) will co-operate with the benign tendencies in human nature and society, wherever found; and that they will, in their degree, be efficacious in making men wiser, better, and happier."

In a subsequent letter to Sir George Beaumont, he says, "Let the poet first consult his own heart, as I have done, and leave the rest to posterity—to, I hope, an improving posterity. . . I have not written down to the level of superficial observers, and unthinking minds. Every great poet is a teacher; I wish either to be considered as a teacher, or nothing."

So far have I tried to prove my point. If my allegations are true, then it follows that a man whose life is choked up by splendour and by riches—a man whose sympathies are perverted by detraction and by gossip—a man whose object is in life to have for himself merely a position in what is called fashionable life—such a a man is simply *incapable* of understanding the highest poetry.

The second qualification I shall name for the appreciation of poetry is, feelings trained and disciplined by the truth of Nature. Let us understand this matter. Poetry represents things, not as they are, but as they seem; and herein it coincides with all high art, for the difference between science and poetry is this—that science and philosophy endeavour to give to us things as they are, art and poetry represent to us things as they seem. Let us take a simple illustration. The painter represents his distant mountains blue, he gives us the distant circle in the oval of perspective, not because they are so, but because they seem so.

Now, in the same way, just as there are perverted senses to which all things seem unreal, and diseased or morbid senses to which, for example, there is no difference between green and scarlet, and as a man who has represented the glaring and glittering as beautiful, would yet find many who admired him, so, in the same way, in a matter of taste or poetry, there will be found minds perverted by convention, or injured by mere position, to whom Humanity and the Universe will not appear in their true colours, but rather falsely. Mere poets of fashion will have their admirers, just so far as there are those who are found like them, and just so far as their powers are great. For it must be remembered that if a thing seems such to a man, and he has the art of representing it as it seems, he is a great poet in the first instance, and if a man has that power to an eminent degree, he is a greater poet; but the question whether he is a true poet or not depends not upon *how* what he represented appeared to him, but upon the question whether it *ought* so to have appeared to him, or whether it does so appear to human nature in its most unsophisticated and purest mood. Then comes the difficulty; what shall be the test? If things seem to one man thus, and if they seem to another man thus, who shall tell us which is true and which is false poetry, and bring us back to a standard by which we may determine what is the judgment of human nature in its most unsophisticated mood? The tests are two. The first is feelings disciplined by Nature, the second is feelings disciplined through the minds of the acknowledged great masters and poets. The first test I have named is feelings disciplined by Nature; for as in matters of art, there are a variety of tastes; it does not necessarily follow that there is no real test or standard of taste.

And just as the real standard is not the standard of the mass—is not judged by the majority of votes, but is decided by the few—so, in matters of poetry, it is not by the mass or by the majority of votes that these things can be tested; but they are to be tested by the pure, and simple, and true in heart—by those who, all their life long, have been occupied in the discipline of feeling; for in early life poetry is a love, a passion; we care not for quality, we care only for quantity; the majesty and pomp of diction delight us; we love the mere mellifluous flow of the rhyme; and this any one will understand who has heard the boy in the playground spouting, in schoolboy phraseology, his sonorous verses. And so, as life goes on, this passion passes; the love for poetry wanes, the mystic joy dies with our childhood, and other and more real objects in life and business occupy our attention. After twenty a man no longer loves poetry passionately, and at fifty or sixty, if you apply to a man for his judgment, you will find it to be that which was his when a boy. The thirty years that have intervened have been spent in undisciplined feeling, and the taste of the boy is still that of the man—imperfect and undisciplined.

The other test to which I will refer is the judgment of the mind that has been formed on the highest models. The first test I have spoken of is, of course, Nature seen and felt at first hand; the second test is Nature seen through the eyes of those who by universal consent are reckoned to have seen Nature best; and without these it is utterly impossible that a man can judge well.

"These two things, contradictory as they seem, must go together—manly dependence and manly independence, manly reliance and manly self-reliance. Nor can there be given to a thinking man any higher or wiser rule than this—to trust to the judgment of those who from all ages have been reckoned great; and if he finds that any disparity or difference exists between his judgment and theirs, let him, in all modesty, take it for granted that the fault lies in him and not in them; for, as a great poet interprets himself to us, he is himself necessary to himself, and we must love him ere to us he will seem worthy of our love." These lines are Wordsworth's, and of no man are they more true than of himself. If you come to Wordsworth in order to find fault, and criticize, and discover passages that can be turned into ridicule or parodied, you will find abundant materials for your mood; but if, on the other hand, in reliance on the judgment of some of the best and wisest of this age, you will take it for granted that there is something there to learn, and that he can and will teach you how to think and how to feel, I answer for it you will not go away disappointed.

And here lies the great difficulty, the peculiar difficulty of our age; that it is an age of cant without love, of criticism without reverence. You read the magazines, and the quarterlies, and the daily newspapers, you see some slashing article, and after you have perused that article, in which the claims of some great writer have been discussed cursorily and superficially, you take it for granted that you understand, and can form a judgment upon the matter; and yet, all the while, very likely that article has been written by some clever, flippant young man, to whom, for his own misfortune, and for the misfortune of the public, the literary department has been committed. What we want is the old spirit of our forefathers; the firm conviction that not by criticism, but by sympathy, we must understand; what we want is more reverence, more love, more humanity, more depth.

The third qualification I shall name for an appreciation of poetry is, a certain delicacy and depth of feeling. I do not say that this is necessary for all poets,—nay, even for some of the highest it is not necessary; for the epic poet appeals to all minds, he describes things which are applicable to all; the dramatic poet appeals to all, because, although unquestionably some of his characters move in an atmosphere that is unintelligible to the mass, yet in the multiplicity of characters he produces there must be a majority that are intelligible to all; the poet of passion appeals to all, because passions are common to us all. It does not require, for example, much delicacy or profoundness to understand and feel the writings of Anacreon Moore; but there are poets who give us truths which none can appreciate but those who have been engaged in watching faithfully the order in which feelings succeed each other, the successions of our inner life, the way in which things appear in this world when presented to our mind in our highest state. No man needs this discipline and preparation more than the student of Wordsworth, for he gives to us the subtle and pure and delicate and refined succession of human feelings, of which the mind is scarcely conscious, except at the moment when the figure is before us, and we are listening with stilled breath to the mysterious march of our inner life.

I will now proceed to give you a few examples of this; but you will observe that I labour under peculiar disadvantages in doing so; for just in proportion as thoughts are delicate, and refined, and subtle, exactly in the same proportion are they unfit for public exposition; they may be fitted for the closet, the study, and for private reading, but they are not fitted for a public room; therefore, the most exquisite productions of Wordsworth I shall not bring before you now; all I shall read to you will be some that will give you a conception of what I have stated. For example, I quote one passage in which the poet describes the consecrating effects of early dawn:—

"What soul was his when from the naked top
Of some bold headland he beheld the sun
Rise up and bathe the world in light! He look'd—
Ocean and earth, the solid frame of earth
And ocean's liquid mass, beneath him lay
In gladness and deep joy. The clouds were touch'd,
And in their silent faces did he read
Unutterable love. Sound needed none,
Nor any voice of joy; his spirit drank
The spectacle; sensation, soul, and form

All melted into him; They swallowed up
His animal being; In them did he live,
And by them did he live; They were his life.
In such access of mind, in such high hour
Of visitation from the Living God.
Thought was not; in enjoyment it expired;
No thanks he breathed, he proffered no request;
Rapt into still communion that transcends
The imperfect offices of prayer and praise,
His mind was a thanksgiving to the Power
That made him; it was blessedness and love!"

There is nothing in these lines except we have the heart to feel them. No man can understand or feel those lines who has led a slothful life, or who has not at one time or other loved to rise early,—no man who, in his early walks, has not mingled with a love of poetry a deep religious sense, who has not felt the consecrating effects of early dawn, or who has not at one time or another, in his early days, in a moment of deep enthusiasm, knelt down amidst the glories of Nature, as the ancient patriarch knelt, canopied only by the sky above him, and feeling that none were awake but the Creator and himself,—bowed down to consecrate and offer up the whole of his life, experiencing also a strange, and awful, and mysterious feeling, as if a Hand invisible was laid upon his brow, accepting the consecration and the sacrifice.

In order to understand the next passage I shall quote, I must remind you of the way in which the ancient Pagans represented the same feeling Most persons here, either through the originals, if they are acquainted with them, or through the translations, which in these times have multiplied, will remember how the ancient Pagan poets loved to represent some anecdote of a huntsman or shepherd, who, in passing through a wood and plucking some herb, or cutting down some branch, has started to see drops of human blood issue from it, or at hearing a human voice proclaiming that he had done injury to some imprisoned human life in that tree. It was so that the ancients expressed their feelings of the deep sacredness of that life that there is in Nature. Now, let us see how Wordsworth expresses this. As usual, and as we might have expected, he brings it before us by a simple anecdote of his childhood, when he went out nutting. He tells us how, in early boyhood, he went out to seek for nuts, and came to a hazel-tree set far in the thicket of a wood, which never had been entered by the profane steps of boyhood before—as he expresses it, "A virgin scene." He describes how he eyed with delight the clusters of white nuts hanging from the branches, and with exquisite fidelity to nature,—he tells us how he sat upon a bank and dallied with the promised feast, as we dally with a letter long expected, and containing correspondence much loved, because we know it is our own. At last the boy rose, tore down the boughs, and on seeing all the ravage and desolation he had caused by his intrusion, there came over him a feeling of deep remorse.

> "And unless I now
> Confound my present feelings with the past;
> Ere from the mutilated bower I turned
> Exulting, rich beyond the wealth of kings,
> I felt a sense of pain when I beheld
> The silent trees, and saw the intruding sky.—
> Then, dearest maiden, move along these shades
> In gentleness of heart; with gentle hand
> Touch—for there is a spirit in the wood."

I preface the third illustration that I shall offer, by a remark reminding you that these scenes of Nature become, as it were, a possession of the memory. The value of having felt Nature in her loveliness or in her grandeur is not in the pleasure and intense enjoyment that was then and there experienced, but in this fact, that we have thenceforward gained something that will not be put aside; a remembrance that will form a great part of our future life. Now, all of us,—any man who has seen the Alps, or who has seen an American hurricane, can understand this so far as Nature's grandeur is concerned; but Wordsworth, as usual, shows us how our daily life and most ordinary being is made up of such recollections; and, as usual, he selects a very simple anecdote to illustrate this. It is taken from a circumstance that occurred to him when on a journey with his sister on the lake of Ullswater, they came upon a scene which, perhaps, few but himself would have observed. The margin of the lake was fringed for a long distance with golden daffodils,

> "Fluttering and dancing in the breeze."

And then, after describing this in very simple language, these lines occur:—

> "The waves beside them danced; but they
> Outdid the sparkling waves in glee;
> A poet could not but be gay,
> In such a jocund company;
> I gazed—and gazed—but little thought
> What wealth the show to me had brought:
>
> "For oft, when on my couch I lie,
> In vacant or in pensive mood,
> They flash upon that inward eye,
> Which is the bliss of solitude;
> And then my heart with pleasure fills,
> And dances with the daffodils."

Now, I will give you a specimen of shallow criticism. In a well-known "Review" for the current quarter there is a review of Wordsworth; and among other passages there is one in which the reviewer, with a flippancy which characterizes the whole of the article, remarks that the passage which has just been read is nothing more than a versified version of a certain entry in Miss Wordsworth's journal. How stands the fact? It is unquestionably true that there was an entry in Miss Wordsworth's journal, written in very striking prose, of the same sight which her brother and herself had seen; it is quite true that the first two stanzas and the greater part of the third were nothing more than Miss Wordsworth's very beautiful prose put into very beautiful verse. So far then, if you strike off the last stanza and the two lines of the stanza preceding it, you have nothing more than a versified version of the entry in Miss Wordsworth's journal; but then, the last stanza contains the very idea of all, towards which all tended, and without which the piece would not have been poetry at all. What would you think of a man who denied to Shakspeare the praise of originality, on the ground that his plays were chiefly constructed from some ancient chronicler, Holingshed, for example, or taken from the plot of some old play, and that in every play he had incorporated some hundred lines of the old play? What has Shakspeare added? Only the *genius;* he has only added the breath and life which made the dry bones of the skeleton live. What has Wordsworth added? He has added nothing except the *poetry;* nothing but the thought, the one lovely thought, which redeems the whole.

Now, I have quoted the passages you have heard, in order to call your attention to the subtle perception and the exquisite delicacy which is in them. I have reminded you of the difficulty I encounter in bringing them before a public audience. In reading Wordsworth the sensation is as the sensation of the pure water drinker, whose palate is so refined that he can distinguish between rill and rill, river and river, fountain and fountain, as compared with the obtuser sensation of him who has destroyed the delicacy of his palate by grosser libations, and who can distinguish no difference between water and water, because to him all pure things are equally insipid. It is like listening to the mysterious music in the conch sea shell, which is so delicate and refined that we are uncertain whether it is the music and sound of the shell, or merely the pulses throbbing in our own ear; it is like watching the quivering rays of fleeting light that shoot up to heaven as we are looking at the sunset; so fine, so exquisitely touching is the sense of feeling, that we doubt whether it is reality we are gazing upon at all, or whether it is not merely an image created by the power and the trembling of our own inner imagination.

I will pass on, now, in the second place, to consider the life of Wordsworth, so far as it may be considered to have affected his poetry. We all know that Wordsworth was remarkable for certain theories of poetry, which, in his time, when they first appeared, were considered new, heterodox, heretical. On a future occasion I hope to examine these; at present, I am bound to endeavour to investigate the question, how far Wordsworth's life and Wordsworth's character may be supposed to have formed, or, at all events, modified, these conclusions.

Now, first of all, I will remark that Wordsworth's was a life of contemplation, not of action, and therein differed from Arnold's of Rugby. Arnold of Rugby is the type of English action; Wordsworth is the type of English thought. If you look at the portraits of the two men, you will distinguish this difference. In one there is concentrativeness, energy, proclaimed; in the eye of the other there is vacancy, dreaminess. The life of Wordsworth was the life of a recluse. In these days it is the fashion to talk of the dignity of work as the one sole aim and end of human life, and foremost in proclaiming this as a great truth we find Thomas Carlyle. Every man who pretends in any degree to have studied the manifold tendencies of this age will be familiar with the writings of Carlyle, and there can be no man who has studied them who does not recollect the vivid and eloquent passage in which Carlyle speaks of the sacredness of work. Now, it appears to me, that this word is passing almost into cant among the disciples of Carlyle; and even with Carlyle himself in these Latter-day pamphlets, in which he speaks of every thing and every one not engaged in present work, as if the sooner they were out of this work-a-day world the better. In opposition to this, I believe that as the vocation of some is naturally work, so the vocation, the heaven-born vocation of others, is naturally contemplation.

In very early times human life was divided into seven parts, whereof six were given to work and one to rest, and both of these were maintained equally sacred—sacred work and sacred rest; and it is not uprooting that great principle, but carrying it out in its spirit, to say—that as of the seven parts of human life the majority belonged to work, so should a fraction be dedicated to rest; that though it is true of the majority that the life-law is work, yet it is also true that there is a fraction to whom by nature the life-law is the law of contemplation. But let no one suppose that contemplation, in the Wordsworthian sense of the word, is listlessness or inaction. There is a sweat of the brain, and a sweat of the heart, be well assured — working-men especially — as much as there is a sweat of the brow; and contemplation, in Wordsworth's sense of the word, is the dedicating a life to the hard and severe inner work of brain; it is the retiring from the world, in order to fit the spirit to do its work.

Let us understand what this work was which Wordsworth proposed to himself. At the period when Wordsworth came upon the stage, there were two great tendencies—and, in some respects, evil tendencies—which civilization and modern society were beginning to develope. The first of these was the accumulation of wealth; the second was the division of labour.

I am not going to speak of the accumulation of wealth as a fanatic. I know some who say with reference to wealth and capital, that wealth is a necessary ingredient in the production of things, of which labour is the other ingredient, and without which labour will be altogether useless. I know that no nation has ever risen to greatness without accumulated capital; and yet, notwithstanding this, there is a crisis in the history of nations—and a dangerous crisis it is—when the aristocracy of birth has been succeeded by the aristocracy of wealth; and a great historian tells us, that no nation has ever yet reached that crisis, without having *already* begun its downward progress towards deterioration.

There are chiefly, I believe, three influences counteractive of that great danger, accumulated wealth. The first is religion, the second is hereditary rank, and the third is the influence of men of contemplative lives. The first is religion, of which, as belonging to another place, for the sake of reverence, I will not speak here. The second counteracting influence to accumulated wealth is hereditary rank. It is not generally the fashion in the present day to speak highly of rank, much less before the members of an Athenæum or of a Working Man's Institute; it is the fashion, rather, to speak of our common Humanity, and to deprecate Rank; and good and right it is that common Humanity should be dignified, and elevated far above the distinction of convention and all the arbitrary and artificial differences of class; and yet, after all this, in an age when it certainly is not the fashion to speak well of hereditary rank, it is well for us all to remember the advantages that have accrued to us in the past, from that hereditary rank. I will say that Rank is a power in itself more spiritual, because less tangible, than the power of wealth. The man who commands others by the extent of his broad acres, or by the number of his bales of cotton, rules them by a power more degrading and more earthly than he who rules them simply by the *prestige* of long hereditary claims.

You all remember how well Sir Walter Scott has described this power as existing more strongly among the Highlanders of Scotland than in any other nation. In the "Fair Maid of Perth," for example, in the contest between the clans, you will remember how every clansman dedicated himself to certain death for the sake of his chieftain, and how a young man, with no wealth, unknown before, nay, having in himself no intrinsic worth or goodness, obtained a loyalty and devotion that royalty itself could scarcely win; a devotion and love that all the wealth of the burghers of Perth never could have purchased; and you feel that so long as there was such a power in Scotland it was impossible that the burghers of Perth, with all their wealth, could obtain undisputed predominancy. So long as this power exists, the power of wealth has something to be thrown in the scale against it; and therefore it is that, with feelings strong on the side of human progress, and with but little reverence for mushroom rank, I am yet free to acknowledge that I feel sometimes a pang, when I hear or read of the extinction of great names, gray with the hoar of innumerable ages—sorrow, when I read in paper after paper of the passing of great ancestral estates under the hammer of the auctioneer; and for this reason, that in every such case I feel that there is one more sword gone that would have helped us in the battle which we must all fight against the superstitious idolatry of Wealth.

The third counteracting influence is the existence of men of contemplative minds—men of science and philosophy. You may call them useless; but they are men whose vocation elevates them above the existing world, and makes them indifferent to show and splendour, and therefore they can throw their influence and weight in the scale against the aristocracy of wealth. The other evil I have spoken of, I called the division of labour; and here, again, I speak not as a fanatic. Political economists, Adam Smith, for example, tell us that in the fabrication of a pin, from ten to eighteen men are required. One cuts the wire, another draws it, a third points it, three are required to make the head, another to polish it, and it is a separate work even to put the pin into the paper. And now, we know the advantage of all this.

The political economist tells us, that ten such men working together can make in a single day forty or fifty thousand pins, whereas, had they worked separately, they could scarcely have made ten. We all know the advantage of this; we know that a man becomes more expert by directing his whole attention to one particular branch of a trade than by wasting it on many; we know that time is thus saved, which would otherwise be spent in going from one work to another; we know that the inventive faculty is consequently quickened, because a man who is for ever considering one subject only, is also enabled to occupy his attention with the thought as to how the operation can be most simplified. These are great advantages; yet no man can persuade me that with these advantages there are not also great disadvantages to the *inner life* of the man so engaged. We get a perfect pin, but we get most imperfect *men*, for while one man is engaged in polishing the pin, and another is engaged in sharpening it, what have we? We have nothing more in the man than a pin-polisher; we have sacrificed the man to the pin.

In some of the States of Western America, we

are told of men who, by the very facts of their position, are compelled to clear their own ground, to sow and reap it with their own hands, to thatch and build their own cottages, and to break and shoe their own horses, and who give a great deal of attention, notwithstanding, to the consideration of great questions, commercial and political. This is, no doubt, an imperfect society, for every thing is incomplete; and yet travellers tell us that there are nowhere such specimens of Humanity; that the men have not only large brains and large muscles, but both these joined together. On the one hand, then, we have a more complete society and a less complete individual; on the other hand, we have a more complete individual and a less complete society. This is the disadvantage, this is the high price we must pay for all civilization and progress; in the words of Tennyson, "The individual withers, and the world is more and more." And, then, life is so divided; we have the dentist and the oculist, but they are only the dentist and the oculist; we have the clergyman and the farmer, but the farmer knows nothing of the clergyman; and is it not a charge brought against the clergy at this very moment, that they are clergymen and nothing more?

No man felt these two dangers more than

Wordsworth felt them; he felt himself called upon to do battle against the evils of his age; he acknowledged that he had received a commission and consecration; he was, as we have already heard, "a consecrated spirit;" and yet he took a fair and just measure of his own powers; he knew well that his work was not to be done on the platform, in the pulpit, or in the senate. He retired to his own mountains, and there, amidst the regenerating influences of nature, where all was real, he tried to discipline his own heart in order that he might be enabled to look calmly and truly on the manifold aspects of human life. And from that solitude there came from time to time a calm clear voice, calling his countrymen back to simplicity and truth, proclaiming the dignity and the simplicity in feeling of our primitive nature; in opposition to the superstitious idolatry of wealth, proclaiming from time to time that a man's life consists not in the abundance of the things he possesses; in opposition to the danger arising from divided employment and occupations, proclaiming the sanctity of each separate human soul, and asserting, in defiance of the manufacturer, who called men "hands," that every man was not a "hand," but a living soul.

It was in this way that Wordsworth advocated

the truth of poetry. He did a great, and high, and holy work, the value of which must not be calculated nor measured by his success, but by its truth. The work Wordsworth did, and I say it in all reverence, was the work which the Baptist did when he came to the pleasure-laden citizens of Jerusalem to work a reformation; it was the work which Milton tried to do, when he raised that clear, calm voice of his to call back his countrymen to simpler manners and to simpler laws. That was what Wordsworth did, or tried to do; and the language in which he had described Milton might with great truth be applied to Wordsworth himself:—

> "Milton! thou should'st be living at this hour:
> England hath need of thee: she is a fen
> Of stagnant waters: altar, sword, and pen,
> Fireside, the heroic wealth of hall and bower,
> Have forfeited their ancient English dower
> Of inward happiness. We are selfish men;
> Oh! raise us up, return to us again;
> And give us manners, virtue, freedom, power.
> Thy soul was like a star, and dwelt apart:
> Thou hadst a voice whose sound was like the sea;
> Pure as the naked heavens, majestic, free.
> So didst thou travel on life's common way,
> In cheerful godliness; and yet thy heart
> The lowliest duties on herself did lay."

I will now read to you one or two passages in

which Wordsworth shows the power of this life of contemplation. The first I shall read is one written by Wordsworth soon after the Convention of Cintra. According to Wordsworth's view, England had been guilty in that Convention of great selfishness. It appeared to Wordsworth that, instead of using the opportunity given her to ransom Portugal and Spain, she had consulted her own selfishness, and allowed her enemy, the French, to escape with a retreat almost equal to victory. In consequence of this, Wordsworth wrote a tract, in one passage of which he defended himself for pretending to judge of such matters:—He says, "The evidence to which I have made appeal, in order to establish the truth, is not locked up in cabinets, but is accessible to all; as it exists in the bosoms of men—in the appearances and intercourse of daily life—in the details of passing events—and in general history. And more especially in its right import within the reach of him who, taking no part in public measures, and having no concern in the changes of things but as they affect what is most precious in his country and humanity, will doubtless be more alive to those genuine sensations which are the materials of sound judgment. Nor is it to be overlooked, that such a man may have more leisure (and probably will have a stronger inclination) to communicate with the records of past ages."

I will take one other passage, in which, judging of the affairs of Spain with almost perfect nicety, Wordsworth again appealed to the power and right given to him, by contemplation, to judge of such a subject:—

"Not mid the world's vain objects, that enslave
The free-born soul—that world whose vaunted skill
In selfish interest perverts the will,
Whose factions lead astray the wise and brave—
Not there; but in dark wood, and rocky cave,
And hollow vale, which foaming torrents fill
With omnipresent murmur as they rave
Down their steep beds, that never shall be still:
Here, mighty nature! in this school sublime,
I weigh the hopes and fears of suffering Spain,
For her consult the auguries of time;
And through the human heart explore my way,
And look and listen—gathering, whence I may,
Triumph and thoughts no bondage can restrain."

The second great feature in Wordsworth's life and history was his fidelity to himself. Early in life he felt himself a consecrated spirit, bound to be such, else sinning greatly. He said that he made no vows, but that, unknown to him, vows were made for him. Wordsworth felt that he had what we call in modern times a vocation or a mission, and no man was ever more true to his vocation than Wordsworth; he was not disobedient to the heavenly vision; he recognized the voice within him and obeyed it; and no wish for popularity, no dazzling invitations to a brighter life, could ever make him break his vows or leave his solitude. The generosity of a few private friends,—Calvert, Beaumont, Lord Lonsdale,—enabled him to live in retirement; but when he was afterwards invited to leave his seclusion for a town life he refused, because he felt that that would destroy the simplicity he was cultivating.

Wordsworth was no copyist; upon himself he formed himself. He took no model; he took the powers and light which were in him, and worked them out. This will account for what some writers called the fanatical egotism of the Lake writers. Egotism, if you will; but there is many a man who is wasting his energies who has, nevertheless, the power within him to be something, if he will only not try to be something which he cannot be—if he will only be content to be what he is within himself, instead of aiming at some model it is impossible for him ever to realize. Abstractedly, no doubt, the armour of the warrior was better than the sling of the shepherd; but for the shepherd the shepherd's sling was best. And so Wordsworth worked out his history, destiny, and life; and, after all, when you look at it, in his case, it was not egotism. Wordsworth said that he made no vows; vows were made for him. And here is the difference between the egotist and the humility of the great man; the egotist is ever speaking and thinking of that which belongs to himself alone and comes from himself; but the great man, when speaking of himself, or thinking of himself, is convinced that which is in him is not his own, but a Voice to which he must listen, and to which, at his peril, he must yield obedience. There has ever been to me something exceedingly sublime in the spectacle of Wordsworth, through obloquy, through long years, through contempt, still persevering in his calm, consistent course—something sublime in those expressions which afterwards turned out to be a prophecy, in which, indifferent to present popularity, he looked towards the future. His friends, who loved him, his brothers, who adored him, were unsatisfied with the public opinion. "Make yourselves at rest respecting me," said Wordsworth; "I speak the truths the world must feel at last." There are not many passages in Wordsworth's Works that bear upon his feelings during this time, and there is only one passage I will read to you now It is that ode he wrote to Haydon:—

"High is our calling, friend!—Creative art
(Whether the instrument of words she use,
Or pencil pregnant with ethereal hues,)
Demands the service of a mind and heart,
Though sensitive, yet, in their weakest part,
Heroically fashioned—to infuse
Faith in the whispers of the lonely muse,
While the whole world seems adverse to desert.
And, oh! when nature sinks, as oft she may,
Through long-lived pressure of obscure distress,
Still to be strenuous for the bright reward,
And in the soul admit of no decay,
Brook no continuance of weak-mindedness:
Great is the glory, for the strife is hard!"

This brings me to consider Wordsworth in his success as a poet. The cause of Wordsworth, which was desperate once, is triumphant now; and yet it is well to look back to fifty years ago, and to remember how it was with him then. Wordsworth's biographer informs us that between 1807 and 1815 there was not one edition of his works called for. The different reviews sneered at him, Jeffrey lashed him, Byron tried to annihilate him; and it was in reference to some such attempt of Byron that Southey said, "He crush the Excursion! he might as well attempt to crush Mount Skiddaw!" It was about that time that Fox returned a calm, cold, unsympathizing answer to the enclosure of a volume of Wordsworth's poems which Wordsworth had sent; and then also occurred one circumstance which was full of signification. Cottle, the bookseller, of Bristol, made over his stock and effects to the Messrs. Longman, and it was necessary to take an inventory of the stock, and in that inventory was found one volume noted down as worth "*nil.*" That volume contained the lyric poems of Wordsworth; and it may be well, also, to say that it contained first of all Coleridge's poem of the "Ancient Mariner," and afterwards those exquisite lines of Wordsworth on "Revisiting Tintern Abbey."

Thirty years after this, the then Prime Minister of England, Sir Robert Peel, in a letter full of dignified, and touching, and graceful feeling, proffered to Wordsworth the Laureateship of England; acknowledging, in addition, that though he had mentioned the subject not to few, but to many persons, and not to men of small, but to men of great reputation, there was but one unanimous opinion, that the selection was the only one that could be made.

I remember myself one of the most public exhibitions of this change in public feeling. It was my lot, during a short university career, to witness a transition and a reaction, or revulsion, of public feeling, with respect to two great men whom I have already mentioned and contrasted. The first of these was one who was every inch a man—Arnold of Rugby. You will all recollect how in his earlier life Arnold was covered with suspicion and obloquy; how the wise men of his day charged him with latitudinarianism, and I know not with how many other heresies. But the public opinion altered, and he came to Oxford and read lectures on Modern History. Such a scene had not been seen in Oxford before. The lecture-room was too small; all adjourned to the Oxford theatre; and all that was most brilliant, all that was most wise and most distinguished, gathered together there. He walked up to the rostrum with a quiet step and manly dignity. Those who had loved him when all the world despised him, felt that, at last, the hour of their triumph had come. But there was something deeper than any personal triumph they could enjoy; and those who saw him then will not soon forget the lesson read to them by his calm, dignified, simple step,—a lesson teaching them the utter worthlessness of unpopularity, or of popularity, as a test of manhood's worth.

The second occasion was when, in the same theatre, Wordsworth came forward to receive his honorary degree. Scarcely had his name been pronounced, than from three thousand voices at once, there broke forth a burst of applause, echoed and taken up again and again when it seemed about to die away, and that thrice repeated—a cry in which

> "Old England's heart and voice unite,
> Whether she hail the wine cup or the fight,
> Or bid each hand be strong, or bid each heart be light."

There were young eyes there, filled with an emotion of which they had no need to be ashamed; there were hearts beating with the proud feeling of triumph, that, at last, the world had recognized the merit of the man they had loved so long, and acknowledged as their teacher; and yet, when that noise was protracted, there came a reaction in their feelings, and they began to perceive that *that* was not, after all, the true reward and recompense for all that Wordsworth had done for England; it seemed as if all that noise was vulgarizing the poet; it seemed more natural and desirable, to think of him afar off in his simple dales and mountains, the high priest of Nature, weaving in honoured poverty his songs to liberty and truth, than to see him there clad in a scarlet robe and bespattered with applause. Two young men went home together, part of the way in silence, and one only gave expression to the feelings of the other when he quoted those well-known, trite, and often-quoted lines,—lines full of deepest truth—

> "The self-approving hour whole worlds outweighs
> Of stupid starers and of loud huzzas;
> And more true joy Marcellus exiled feels
> Than Cæsar with a senate at his heels."

The last thing I shall remark on respecting Wordsworth's life was Wordsworth's consistency. I shall here quote a passage in which he alludes to the charge brought against him of having deserted his former opinions. "I should think that I had lived to little purpose if my notions on the subject of government had undergone no modification: my youth must, in that case, have been without enthusiasm, and my manhood endued with small capability of profiting by reflection. If I were addressing those who have dealt so liberally with the words renegade, apostate, &c. I should retort the charge upon them, and say, *you* have been deluded by *places* and *persons*, while I have stuck to *principles*." It may appear to many persons a desperate thing to defend Wordsworth's consistency in the very teeth of facts; for it is unquestionable that in his early life Wordsworth was a Republican, and sympathized with the French Revolution, and that in his later life he wrote lines of stern condemnation for its excesses. It is unquestionable, moreover, that in early life Wordsworth rebelled against any thing like ecclesiastical discipline; that he could not even bear the morning and evening prayers at chapel, and yet that in later life he wrote a large number of Ecclesiastical sonnets, of which I will at present only quote one on Archbishop Laud—

"Prejudged by foes determined not to spare
An old weak man for vengeance thrown aside,
Laud, 'in the painful art of dying' tried,
(Like a poor bird entangled in a snare,
Whose heart still flutters, though his wings forbear
To stir in useless struggle,) hath relied
On hope that conscious innocence supplied,
And in his prison breathes celestial air.
Why tarries then thy chariot? wherefore stay,
O Death! the ensanguined yet triumphant wheels,
Which thou preparest, full often to convey
(What time a state with maddening faction reels)
The saint or patriot to the world that heals
All wounds, all perturbations doth allay." *

* Wordsworth appended to this sonnet the following note, which is given entire to show the strength of his opinion on this subject:—

"In this age a word cannot be said in praise of Laud, or even in compassion for his fate, without incurring a charge of bigotry; but fearless of such imputation, I concur with Hume, 'that it is sufficient for his vindication to observe that his errors were the most excusable of all those which prevailed

So that Wordsworth began as a Republican and ended as a Tory; he began in defiance of every thing ecclesiastical, and ended as a High Churchman. This change has been viewed by persons of different parties with different sentiments. To some, as to the poet Shelley, it appeared an apostasy from the purity of his earlier principles; to others, as if the sacredness of his earlier principles had been ripened with the mellowed strength of manly life. Among these last is his biographer, Dr. Wordsworth; and it is curious to see what pains he has taken to point to some passage by which the evil of another might be modified—aiming at one great and chief object, namely, to prove that Wordsworth died a Tory

during that zealous period.' A key to the right understanding of those parts of his conduct that brought the most odium upon him in his own time, may be found in the following passage of his speech before the bar of the House of Peers: 'Ever since I came in place, I have laboured nothing more than that the external publick worship of God, so much slighted in divers parts of this kingdom, might be preserved, and that with as much decency and uniformity as might be. For I evidently saw, that the publick neglect of God's service in the outward face of it, and the nasty lying of many places dedicated to that service, *had almost cast a damp upon the true and inward worship of God, which, while we live in the body, needs external helps, and all little enough to keep it in any vigour.*'"

and a High Churchman. Be it so; I am prepared to say that the inner life of Wordsworth was consistent. In order to prove this, let us bear in mind that there are two kinds of truth—the one is the truth of fact, the other is ideal truth; and these are not one, they are often opposite to each other. For example, when the agriculturist sees a small white almond-like thing rising from the ground, he calls that an oak; but that is not a truth of fact, it is an ideal truth. The oak is a large tree, with spreading branches, and leaves, and acorns; but that is only a thing an inch long, and imperceptible in all its development; yet the agriculturist sees in it the idea of what it shall be, and, if I may borrow a scriptural phrase, he *imputes* to it the majesty, and excellence, and glory, that is to be hereafter.

Let us carry this principle into the change of Wordsworth's principles. In early life Wordsworth was a democrat; an admirer of the French Revolution; he sympathized deeply, manfully, with the cause of the poor; he loved them, and desired their elevation. But he sympathized with them as the stately nobles of nature; he saw in them, not what they were, but what they might be; and in all Wordsworth's peddlers, and broom-gatherers, and gypsies, and wanderers, we have not bad men, defiled by crime; but there is, speaking though them all, the high, pure mind of Wordsworth. He simply exhibited his own humanity, which he felt and knew to be in them also. This is an ideal truth and not a truth of fact, and the idea is not what they were, but what they ought to be, and what they yet should be.

Let us, again, on the other hand, come to the question of Wordsworth's change into High Churchism and Toryism. And first, by the way, I would remark that there is another side of the truth Wordsworth put forward, which you will find in a poem familiar to most of you, in which Canning has given us the history of the "Needy Knife Grinder." A republican, in all the warmth of republican spirit, with his lips full of liberty, fraternity, and equality, sees approaching, a man in rags—a poor wretched looking being; and he instantly imagines that here is some victim to the oppression of the Poor Laws, the Game Laws, or of Tithes, or Taxation; but it turns out, upon inquiry, that he has before him a man of bad life, of indolent and intemperate habits, who, in a fit of intoxication, has got into the wretched state in which he beholds him; and the indignation and confusion of our good republican are completed when the Needy Knife Grinder entreats that he would give him some small coin, in order that he might become drunk again. This is the other side of truth—the truth of fact —a low, and base, and vulgar truth. And, after all, when we come to examine these, which is the higher truth?—is it higher to state things as they really are, or to state them as they ought to be?—to say that the lower classes are degraded, and evil, and base; or to say that there yet slumbers in them the aristocratic and the godlike, and that *that*, by the grace of God, shall one day be drawn forth? In early life, then, in all his most democratic feelings, Wordsworth was an aristocrat at heart.

And now we come to the other side of the question. And first, in reference to the term "High Churchism," I do not use it in an offensive sense. If there are any persons here holding High Church views, I implore them to believe that, although I am not a High Churchman myself—far from it—I can yet sympathize with them in all their manliness and high-mindedness; and recognize much in them that is pure and aspiring. If, therefore, I now give my own definition of High Churchism, let them not be offended. There are, then, two things opposite to each other; the one is Pantheism, the other is High Churchism. Pantheism is a tendency to see the godlike everywhere, the personal God nowhere. The other, is the tendency to localize the personal Deity in certain places, certain times, and certain acts; certain places called consecrated churches; certain times called fast-days, and so forth; certain acts, called acts of ecclesiastical life, in certain persons, called consecrated priests. These two things, you will observe, are opposed to each other—diametrically opposed. Now, it is a strange and remarkable fact, that Wordsworth has been charged with both these things; by some he has been charged with Pantheism, and by others with what we call High Churchism. In reference to Pantheism, in order that those who are not familiar with the word may understand it, I will quote one or two passages from Wordsworth. The first, which occurs in the sonnets, I have read. In that it will be seen that Wordsworth speaks of the force of Nature as if that were the only living Soul of the world. I will take another passage which occurs in the well-known lines on Revisiting Tintern Abbey:—

"And I have felt
A presence that disturbs me with the joy
Of elevated thoughts; a sense sublime
Of something far more deeply interfused,
Whose dwelling is the light of setting suns,
And the round ocean, and the living air,

And the blue sky, and in the mind of man:
A Motion and a Spirit, that impels
All thinking things, all objects of all thought,
And rolls through all things."

In these words, grand and magnificent as they are, we have the very germ of Pantheism. But now, in looking at one of these classes of passages, we must ever remember to modify it by the other. When Wordsworth spoke as a High Churchman, we must remember that he was the very same man who spoke of the Living Being that created the universe, as "A Motion and a Spirit that impels all thinking things;" and when, on the other hand, I use language which seems to pass almost into Pantheism, we must remember that he was the same man who wrote the Ecclesiastical sonnets, and who spoke of a personal and localized Deity.

And what if it be true,—and true it is,—that the earlier part of Wordsworth's life was characterized by the predominancy of one of these feelings, and the later part by the other—is there any thing there that is unnatural or inconsistent? Is it unnatural if the mind of a man progresses from the vague transcendental down towards the personal? Is there any thing inconsistent in the great truth, that the mind of man, after having wandered in the outer confines of the circumference of this universe, should at last seek its home and find its blessedness in the rest of a personal centre? Now, with respect to the other point, namely, Wordsworth's Toryism, or Conservatism—call it what you will; it does not matter whether I am now addressing Tories or Radicals; since we are speaking of great principles we will have done with names. I will read you a passage in which Wordsworth speaks of England:—

"Hail to the crown by freedom shaped—to gird
An English sovereign's brow! and to the throne
Whereon he sits. Whose deep foundations lie
In veneration and the people's love;
Whose steps are equity, whose seal is law."

Now, the veriest democrat can only object to this as a matter of fact, and will probably say, "If this be England I would desire to preserve her as she is; but because I do not believe it, I desire to alter her; in heart and in idea we are one, the only point on which we differ is the point of historical fact." I say, therefore, that in Wordsworth's most democratic days he was aristocratic in heart; and in his most aristocratic days he had all that was most generous, and all that was most aspiring in the democratic mind. I now come rapidly towards the conclusion; but having said what I have, it is necessary that I should complete the picture by giving you an idea of the patriotism in Wordsworth; that intense and deep love for England, in which aristocrat and democrat are blended in the formation of one high-minded man. I will read a passage showing Wordsworth's love for his country:—

> "When I have borne in memory what has tamed
> Great nations, how ennobling thoughts depart
> When men change swords for legers, and desert
> The student's bower for gold, some fears unnamed
> I had, my country!—am I to be blamed,
> Now, when I think of thee, and what thou art,
> Verily in the bottom of my heart,
> Of those unfilial fears I am ashamed.
> For dearly must we prize thee; we who find
> In thee a bulwark for the cause of men;
> And I by my affection was beguiled:
> What wonder if a poet now and then,
> Among the many movements of his mind,
> Felt for thee as a lover or a child?"

I must preface the next sonnet I have to read, by reminding you, that it was written at a period when a French invasion was expected. It is a very hard and difficult thing for us in the present day, broken as we are into so many factions, to conceive the united enthusiasm which stirred the heart of England in those days, when every moment the invasion of the great conqueror of

Europe was possible. The fleets of England swept the seas; on every hill the signal beacons blazed; 420,000 men were in arms; the service of the church was liable to be interrupted by the clang of arms upon the pavement; every village churchyard was converted into a parade-ground; every boy felt as if there were strength, even in his puny arm, to strike a blow in defence of the cause of his country; every man, excepting when he thought of the women of his country, was longing for the time to come, when it should be seen with what a strength, with what a majesty a soldier fought, when he was fighting in the magnificent and awful cause of his altar and his hearth.

The moment was like that of the deep silence which precedes a thunder-storm, when every breath is hushed, and every separate dried leaf, as it falls through the boughs, is heard tinkling, tinkling down through the branches, from branch to branch; when men's breath was held; when men's blood beat thick in their hearts, as if they were waiting in solemn and grand, but not in painful—rather in triumphant—expectation for the moment when the storm should break, and the French cry of "Glory" should be thundered back again by England's sublimer battle-cry of "Duty!" It was at this time that Wordsworth's sonnet appeared:—

"It is not to be thought of that the flood
Of British freedom, which to the open sea
Of the world's praise, from dark antiquity
Hath flowed, with 'pomp of waters unwithstood,'
Roused though it be full often to a mood
Which spurns the check of salutary bands,
That this most famous stream in bogs and sands
Should perish! and to evil and to good
Be lost for ever. In our halls is hung
Armoury of the invincible Knights of old:
We must be free or die, who speak the tongue
That Shakspeare spake; the faith and morals hold
Which Milton held. In every thing we are sprung
Of earth's first blood, have titles manifold."

In the next passage I have to bring before you, I will remind you of some other facts. The sonnet is addressed to the men of Kent. Now, there is a difference between the Kentish men and the men of Kent. The Kentish men are simply the inhabitants of the county of Kent. The "Men of Kent" is a technical expression applied to the inhabitants of that part of Kent who were never subdued in the Norman invasion, and who obtained glorious terms for themselves, on capitulation, receiving the confirmation of their own charters; so that until very recently—if not at present—they were still in possession of the custom called Gavelkind, by which the sons inherited, not unequally, the eldest taking precedence, but they all taking share and share alike. It was to the "Men of Kent," the inhabitants of that part of the county nearest to the neighbouring land of France, that Wordsworth addressed this sonnet:—

> "Vanguard of Liberty, ye Men of Kent,
> Ye children of a soil that doth advance
> Her haughty brow against the coast of France,
> Now is the time to prove your hardiment!
> To France be words of invitation sent!
> They from their fields can see the countenance
> Of your fierce war, may ken the glittering lance,
> And hear you shouting forth your brave intent.
> Left single, in bold parley, ye, of yore,
> Did from the Norman win a gallant wreath;
> Confirmed the charters that were yours before;—
> No parleying now! In Britain is one breath,
> We all are with you now from shore to shore:—
> Ye men of Kent, 'tis victory or death!"

In this age of cosmopolitanism, when we are, forsooth, too much philanthropists to be patriots; when any deep and strong emotion of love to our country is reckoned as nothing more than the sacredness of the schoolboy's affection; when our young people who have travelled can find no words more capable of expressing their contempt than these—"It is so English;" it does the heart good to read these firm and pure, and true and manly words, issuing from the lips of one who was not ashamed to love his country with all his heart, and with all his soul, and with all his mind, and with all his strength; a man whose every word, and every thought, and every act, were the words, and thoughts, and acts, of a manly, true-spirited, high-minded Englishman!

NOTES OF A LECTURE,

&c., &c.

NOTES OF A LECTURE

Delivered at Hurstper-point, in 1851, *to the Members of a Working Man's Reading Room.*

I AM here to-night through the invitation of your kind friends, with no right but that of unfeigned interest in every institution like yours.

The subject I had proposed was the Progress of Society. I changed it for that of the Working Classes. But even this is too full of pretension.

Nevertheless, the mere fact of my standing here to-night is full of significance.

More so than railways or electric telegraphs.

That so many of the Working Classes should come here after a hard day's work is very significant.

It proves the growing victory of the spirit over the animal: That the lower life of toil and animal indulgence is getting to be reckoned as not the *all* of man.

It shows, too, that the Working Classes are becoming conscious of their own destinies.

Any Society is in an advanced state when it begins to contemplate itself, and asks, "Whither do we tend?"

Three thousand years ago, the centre of the World's civilization was in Eastern Africa.

The monuments of this civilization still remain. The Pyramids.——They are the wonder of travellers, whose report of their measurements excites, in turn, our astonishment and surprise.

But to one considering the progress of the race, these Pyramids tell a different tale. They were built by the Working Classes, under coercion. They were built for Royal ostentation.

Herodotus speaks of hundreds of thousands degraded into serfs.

In the Metropolis of the World's present civilization, a structure stood this year almost as marvellous as these pyramids.

Remarkable not for gigantic massiveness.—— But for punctuality and order.

Built, too, under Royal auspices, and built by the Labouring Classes.

But not built, like the pyramids, for Royal splendour. It was built for the exhibition of the works of Labouring Men.

You could not go through that building without feeling that Royalty itself was second there, not first.

One feeling I had was—There is nothing here that I can make. I belong to the non-producing classes.

New era.——The dignity of Labour.——The sinking of the Individual in the Society.

Another truth typified by that bearing on the destinies of the Working Classes. The approach of an age of Peace.——Falaise.——Guizot.

Assume, then, the fact of the growing importance of the Working Classes.

There are two ways of treating this fact, just as there are two ways of treating an heir just entering on a noble patrimony. One is, that of the sycophant, to tell him how great he is.

Another way is, that of wise friends, who tell him that as he has become great, therefore he has duties; because he has become rich, therefore he has responsibilities.

There are two ways of treating the Working Classes. One, to tell them how enlightened they are.——How powerful.——That Vox populi vox Dei, &c.

Another, that of reminding them that because free, they should fit themselves for freedom; because destined to play a great part on the stage of the world's history, therefore it behooves them to cast off their ignorance—their vices.

Value of these Institutions. First, Habits of self-government. Secondly, They expand the sympathies.

I hold it as a principle that a man is great and good in proportion to the extent of his sympathies.—The man whose eye is ever fixed on himself is the smallest of human beings.—The next step is love of Relations.—The next, love of Country.—The next, sympathy with all that belongs to Man.

And this is God's method of gradual education, through the Family, the Nation, the Race.

One means given for this is public newspapers, which tell of other countries.——A wise man gets out of the paltry events of his own village—election of churchwardens, &c.—to think of great questions.——Further still, the social state of other countries.

Observe on our English narrowness, the idea that one Englishman is equal to two Frenchmen. ——We are apt to think that English manners, English literature, &c. is the only good thing in God's World.

Recent case of an illustrious foreigner, formerly Dictator of Hungary. Received with enthusiasm by the Working Classes. I pronounce no opinion in this place about him. Some say great, good, noble, others call him a charlatan and revolutionist. This matters not. The question is not so much *what* a man worships, admires, but *as* what. Kossuth may be no hero, if you will; but to see those hard-handed sons of toil in Manchester and Birmingham honouring one whom they thought good and noble, when in exile and oppressed; he has little heart indeed who is not touched by it.

Now this kind of Institution fits men for Work. ——Foolish objection that it incapacitates them for business.——The labourer who knows something of chemistry—on what principle soils are composed; why such manures are employed in one case and not in another; according to what laws decomposition takes place—is a better labourer than one who knows nothing of all this.

The mechanic who understands the laws of motion, is a better mechanic than the Chinese sort, who can merely follow a copy.

The domestic servant is improved when she understands the reason why certain things are done, and why certain results follow.

There is a foolish prejudice against educating the poor, lest we should fail to get servants or apprentices.

Putting aside the diabolical character of the

objection, think of the sacrifice of a human being, that your work may be done or your food made!

Progress means—1. Not to be free from work; envy of ladies and gentlemen false and foolish, if by that is meant persons who have nothing to do but to amuse themselves.——Laws of Humanity. ——Greatness.——Goodness.——Only through toil is muscular strength and health gained. Mental force is got by struggle with difficulty.

2. Not the obliteration of differences in rank.

There can be no doubt that the growth in importance of the labouring classes will alter ranks, making them less exclusive, less bitter to others—will raise some who are now degraded, &c.

But it betrays an ignorance of human nature to suppose that ranks will ever be obliterated. Superior tastes, capacities, &c. will unite some into a class, and distinguish them from others.

Gradation of ranks bring out various manifestations of our Humanity.——Gratitude.——Aspiration.——Dignity.——Respect.

3. Not the obliteration of difference in condition.

Of the many errors entertained by those who have advocated the cause of the Working Man, there are few to be more regretted than the exaggerated importance attached to inequality of condition.

Inequality of condition, so far as it stints the faculties, or cuts off from opportunities of information, it is well to desire should be removed, but in itself it is a trifle. And all this foolish exaggeration fixes the attention on what is external in the condition, as if the equality to be arrived at were the superficial external equality. It is not this that makes real inequality. False vulgar thoughts that because you cannot keep a horse or drive a carriage, therefore you have not your rights.

4. But progress means increased opportunities of developing the heart, the conscience, and the intellect. It is not each man's born right to be as rich as his neighbour, or to possess the soil.

But it is his inalienable right to be permitted to develope all the powers that God gave.

If the labourer live so that the death of a child is welcomed by the thought that there is one mouth the less to feed, he cannot develope his heart-affections.

If he lives in a cottage where brothers and sisters sleep in one room, he cannot develope his conscience.

If he comes home overworn, so that he has no time to read, then he cannot develope his intellect.

Clearly, therefore, define such a social position for the labouring man as shall give him scope enough to be in every sense of the word a MAN. A Man whose respect is not servility; whose religion is not superstition; and whose obedience is not the drudgery of dumb driven cattle.

Until that time come, the Working Classes are not free.

A SPEECH

Delivered at the Town Hall, Brighton, April 24, 1849, *at a Meeting of the Inhabitants, called by the Early Closing Association, presided over by the Bishop of Chichester.*

The Resolution which has been put into my hands is,—" That this meeting, believing that an earlier and more uniform hour of suspension of business would give time to all engaged therein for moral and intellectual improvement, would recommend to all tradesmen the hour of eight o'clock as the hour of closing throughout the year; and pledges itself to make purchases before eight o'clock in the evenings, and to request their servants to do the same."

There is a vast difference between that which is theoretically desirable, and that which is practically possible. Our enthusiasm is frequently corrected by experience. It throws too wild, too sanguine, a hope on the future. But difficulties arise; and that which at first seemed easy, turns out to be at last an impossibility. It is in almost every undertaking as it is in life. The lesson we have to learn in life is the same lesson which we have to learn in travelling through a mountainous country. The first lesson is, to estimate distances. The traveller sees the mountain summit sparkling in the evening sun, apparently close above his head; and he resolves that the next morning he will ascend that mountain, and come down again before breakfast. But he finds next day a long three miles between himself and the mountain foot; and that when he has arrived there it takes five or six hours to ascend, and half that time to come back again; and it is well if he returns before nightfall. It is precisely the same with every human undertaking. Our first idea is very different from that which attainment teaches us. We set out with brilliant expectations; we find them very slow in realizing themselves. And so life assumes, by degrees, a soberer and a sadder hue. We find that between our ideal and its attainment there is an immense interval. That which seemed to be the work of days we find to be the work of months; that which seemed to be the work of years turns out to be the work of centuries. And so, step by step, man is disenchanted—led on by hopes of a bright future which is never realized *here*. I believe that the lesson of all experience and of all life is this:—to expect very little, for there is but little of human expectation to be attained; to sow abundantly, and to be satisfied with a very small harvest. Happy is the man not thoroughly broken by disappointment! Happy is that man! for the object of this training is, not to discourage him, but that he may work more calmly, with less of fitful enthusiasm—with steady gaze fixed on the Hereafter! I make these observations, because they are peculiarly applicable to the subject in hand. This subject of Early Closing has been taken up by many people very warmly at first, who have cooled down, and have afterwards let it drop. Two or three years ago there was a large meeting in this town for the same purpose as this one. Some of those who were then enthusiastic and earnest have by degrees become lukewarm and despondent. Their expectations have not been realized; much that was hoped for has not been attained; there have been many difficulties which were not anticipated. And so the result has been, that they have fallen back into coldness and indifference. It is for this reason that I think the tone we should adopt this evening should be calm and sober.

It is exceedingly easy to paint this subject in

most glowing colours. It is the easiest thing in the world to represent the young men as craving for intellectual knowledge, as suffering under physical difficulties, as eager for, and requiring moral improvement. It is exceedingly easy to do all this, because there is a great deal of truth in it. It is exceedingly easy, moreover, because it is popular. But I am not here to say that which is popular; but that which is true. I am not here to say that which shall win a cheer; but to say that which shall be practical and useful. We are met here to-night for two purposes. To resolve that "an earlier and more uniform hour of suspension of business would give time to all engaged therein for moral and intellectual improvement;" and that the meeting "recommend to all tradesmen the hour of eight o'clock as the hour of closing throughout the year, and pledges itself to make purchases accordingly." The subject is complicated with difficulties; and although it would be exceedingly easy to speak in denunciation of those opposed to this movement of Early Closing, I feel there is something to be said on both sides of the question; and therefore I ask the meeting to listen to me dispassionately.

In considering this question, we discern three things: the desirable, the difficult, the possible.

With regard to the desirable, I believe it will

be generally admitted that it is desirable for business to be carried on within fewer hours. There is a great difference between the way in which this question is to be looked at, as a manufacturing, and as a trading question. The question touching hours in the factory does not hold good as to the shop. The object of the factory is to produce; and it may be argued that the work done in twelve hours cannot be done in ten. It is not true that this argument can hold with respect to trade. In trade the object is, not to produce materials, but to serve customers; and if you take the shops in which most work is done, there is not one in which there cannot be found five minutes, ten minutes, half hours, hours, in which all employed are not waiting for customers. Let those five minutes and half hours be added up, and they will more than cover the time taken in serving after any given hour, say seven or eight o'clock. If those customers had come in before nine or ten, there is not one in this meeting who will not acknowledge there were people and time enough to serve them. Then all of us will agree in the possibility that the work may be done in less time. That, if it can be done in less time, it should be done, I think will also be agreed; and the resolution furnishes us with the reasons—"that an earlier and more uniform hour of suspension of business would give time to all engaged therein for moral and intellectual improvement."

Into the physical necessity for this early closing I shall not enter. It is a medical question, and I believe that members of the medical profession, who will address you, will touch on this with more effect than I could do. I ask no further proof of the physical necessity which exists, than to see the working man and the assistant in the shop, in their Sunday walk. There is in their gait a languor and an effeminacy which should not belong to Englishmen. In the second place, this matter is necessary for the sake of intellectual improvement. This age has been often called the age of the aristocracy of wealth. The aristocracy of birth is now much passed by. We are living in an age in which gold is worshipped. In former ages, "virtue" was "valour." In Italy, in the present day, the word "vertu," applied to a man, means "taste in amassing curiosities." In England we speak of the worth of a man as proportioned by the amount of gold which he has been enabled to gather round him as a kind of accretion. And, therefore, it is a matter of rejoicing for me to see a meeting which protests against a principle such as this. This meeting proclaims, in the face of the day, that there is something more sublime in man than the worship of gold. It maintains that there is in the nature of man, that which requires and demands intellectual and moral improvement.

Now, with regard to the intellectual improvement, I shall not press it too much. It is perfectly possible that it may be exaggerated. I will not say that all these young men are craving intellectual knowledge. The young men in the trading classes are like the young men in the upper classes; and I suppose that if one out of twenty in either class is earnestly desirous of this intellectual knowledge, it is a large average. I will grant there is not a difficulty in the way of obtaining this knowledge that may not be surmounted. Men borne down by defects of position and education have achieved for themselves intellectual emancipation. Ferguson, Watt, and Franklin, are noble examples of this. There are men who seem to be born intellectual heroes; men born to cut their way through any obstacles, men who only require to meet difficulties in their way, and those difficulties will be surmounted. They are like the trees on the mountain, that require no more than a bare covering of soil on the rock to strike their roots firmly down; nothing more than the clear, serene, thin air of heaven to throw abroad their branches in. These are intellectual giants; and they would acquire knowledge under any circumstances; it is impossible to crush them. But it is not for men like these that I have to plead. The mass of men are not the intellectual giants; they are rather the humble and the feeble; the exotic, that requires care and culture. They require to be fostered, to be placed on the sunny side of the hill. Give them opportunities, give them time; and then it will be found, not that they will attain grand intellectual dimensions, but they will achieve something like intellectual respectability. And I desire to mention one circumstance, which seems to be a strong corroboration of this fact. Some time ago, the drapers of this town resolved on closing at an earlier hour; and about the same time the Brighton ATHENÆUM was established, in order that the young men might have an opportunity of intellectual cultivation; many young men availed themselves of those opportunities. From causes into which I will not now enter, the rule of Early Closing was obliged to be infringed. Ask you the result? At this time, the Athenæum contained something like 600 or 700 members. There are about 200 assistants, I am told, engaged in the Drapery trade in this town; and of these, 60 were members of the Athenæum; all but ten withdrew. I will not press too much on this; I know in some cases there were rooms provided by employers, and libraries furnished, and that these withdrew them from the Athenæum; but I hold the case indisputably to be this, that if there be a time allowed for cultivation of the mind, there is on the part of the young men a real wish to avail themselves of it.

In the next place, this resolution maintains that Early Closing is necessary for "moral improvement." Early closing is necessary for leisure. Man was not made to divide his time between Study and Work. Besides that, there must be Recreation. He who made the eye, spread around us this world of beauty, and caused the contemplation of it to be accompanied by the feeling of intense enjoyment;—He who threw into the heart the power of domestic affection, gave it delight in domestic sympathy;—He who led his disciples into the desert to "rest awhile," made man for recreation. And, therefore, I am prepared to take it on the lowest ground. The young men require, not merely mental instruction, but time for pleasure, for social enjoyment, for recreation. It is partly for this purpose the Sabbath is necessary for man. It is necessary, in the first place, to nurse the Human; and, in the second, to nurse the Divine within him. In the first to give to man recreation, and in that he shares with the lowest animals; in the second, the cultivation which should nurse the Divine within him. You have, in the first, necessity for Rest; in the second, necessity for Worship. It is the result of the late closing to make the Sabbath day simply and solely a day of rest, and not of holiness. It may be well to speak of the desecration of the Sabbath day. To say the trains shall not run on Sundays; to say the citizens of London shall not leave their homes, nor the artisan go out of Brighton into the country;—it is easy to say this. But we have no right to say that if a man has not time for rest in the week, he shall not take it on the Sabbath.

Once more. This Early Closing is wanted for moral improvement. For the sake of "work," I draw a distinction between it and "occupation." "Occupation" is not "work." The object, the intention, of occupation is a blessed one. It saves the mind from corrupting and wearing out itself. The man who has nothing to do is a most wretched character. He rises in the morning, with fifteen hours before him, in which he makes society wretched and himself wretched also. There is something else implied in "work." "Work" is productive. It produces something;

it gives to a man's character self-dependence and inward strength. Boswell, with his singular simplicity, tells us of an occasion in which he was overtaken by a storm; and he relates that he went about asking question after question of the sailors, interrupting every man in his duty, till at last a sailor put a rope in his hand, and said, "We are in danger, and the safety of the vessel depends on this being held with great force." Occupied in this way, he forgot his fears; and the storm passed over. He had all the while been pulling a useless rope. His was "occupation;" the sailor's "work" was productive. The artizan is a man engaged in work; he is a man who either cultivates the soil and produces food for man to live upon; or, he takes the raw material, and makes furniture and all things necessary for life. The shopkeeper has not "work," but "occupation;" for no man will tell us that the men engaged all day long in folding and unfolding ribbons, showing them in proper lights, and putting them across the counter—no one will tell us he has been engaged in "work;" he has in "occupation." It has saved himself and society from the wretchedness cast upon idleness. Therefore we claim these hours, that young men may exchange "occupation" for "work." Young men! For what purpose do you ask early hours?

Is it for leisure only?—is it to escape from occupation? If that be all, Brighton is being stirred for a very small cause; whereas the young men who came to me as a deputation, spoke of something far higher. They asked for time; not to give it to leisure only, not to give it to social enjoyment only, but to work, to discipline their minds, to do the great duty God has given them to do on earth, that their soul, and body, and spirit might be presented perfect before their Maker.

And now I come to the second part of what I have to say. Having spoken of the "desirable," I pass on to the "difficult." And the first difficulty arises from the peculiar circumstance of Brighton. Brighton is not a manufacturing town, neither is it a commercial town. Brighton is a place of enjoyment for strangers. Something like one third or one fourth will be found not to be residents, but extraneous of the population. Every Saturday, London pours out thousands to take advantage of the sea air. Let any man go to the railway station, and he will be astonished to see the mass of human beings flocking into the town. What is the result? Numbers come down by the last train. They go to the hotels and lodging-houses, and there are articles of consumption wanted. They send out—they must send out—for their provisions; and then, if a tradesman refuses to sell, one difficulty is, that he may have lost a customer for life. There is another difficulty. They go through the place,—through the principal streets of the town; and then, every tradesman knows that during the last two hours of the day, sauntering about there, there are numbers of people who will be induced to go into the shops and purchase the goods which are seen in the brilliantly-lighted windows; and it requires a strong amount of principle for the master tradesman to say he will sacrifice a profit, which, if he does, he will never have in any other way.

Again. The town is the resort of the wealthy—of the aristocracy. There is a difference between this town and manufacturing towns on that account. I have inquired, and I find that, in Sheffield, and Birmingham, and Liverpool, and most places of that kind, the early closing is easily carried out, and carried out at even earlier hours than seven; for in manufacturing towns, life is of a different description. There all men play into each other's hands—all understand each other's necessities. But, at Brighton and Cheltenham, there is a peculiar difficulty; and the difficulty arises partly from this—that the inhabitants are the wealthy. Here, much is different; few understand one another; and when we come to inquire, we find that it is not the purchases of the rich themselves that form the great staple in the occupation of these late hours, but it is the servants of the rich classes. And here I would say a word to mistresses on a subject of which they can necessarily know nothing. I made it my business to make inquiries of the police, and the information given to me by them was of the most appalling character, because it told a sad tale of the result of that which is done in perfect ignorance. When the female servant is sent out at night, the mistress knows not the consequences, nor the sin and misery which often comes from female servants going out at late hours to purchase. I do not say this in a spirit of indignation against those mistresses and employers. It is simply ignorance on their part, not hard-heartedness. But it is a thing to impress upon ourselves and others, that there is

> "An evil wrought by want of thought,
> As well as want of heart."

I pass on to another difficulty; and that arises from the deterioration of the character of the young men themselves. Those who are present now are not the master-tradesmen; or I would take a different course. Those present now are most anxious that the masters should concede this boon of early closing; and therefore I will say, not that which may be popular, but that which may be calculated to do good. In the first place, there is a feeling widely existing, that the use made of this privilege is not what it ought to have been. All the returns of your libraries show how few works of information are read—how many of fiction. More than that, the police tell us that the cigar-shop reaps a terrible harvest out of the wages of the young men; that the billiard-table is at work; that the public-houses, and houses worse than they, are full. I therefore press this matter urgently on the young men. Better far that the hours of business should even be extended, than that extra hours should be gained for licentiousness (so falsely called pleasure), or for mere idleness, which is the grave of a living man. Better, far! for your whole being, physical, moral, and intellectual. Beware, too, of eye-service, for I have it from the master of some of the men, that he has lost confidence in them in respect of their attention to business when not overlooked. The way in which your leaders have acted, and the sentiments they have expressed on this subject, do them great honour. And if the young men used the privilege of early closing on the principle set forth by their leaders, the last difficulty will vanish away.

There is, however, a difficulty in this respect, that it is hardly possible to legislate in an artificial manner. We desire that the shops should be closed at eight. This law, like other laws, will be of advantage, if it be in accordance with the feeling produced already in society; but, if it be superimposed on society, it must fail. Every thing of legislation coercive, and not expressive of the mind and desire of Society, must fail. When England tried to force her Episcopacy on Scotland, the result was, that the Episcopacy was thrown off, never probably to be placed in power there again. When England tried to force Protestantism on Ireland, compulsorily, the result was, that Roman Catholicism became the religion of the land. So with private individuals. The law can never be compulsorily enforced. We must proceed from that which is within to that which is without; and not from that which is without to that which is within. A man of disorderly habits tries to regulate himself by an outward rule; and he sits down and maps out his time and proposes a plan of action, and he has it on his paper beautifully arranged, the books he will read and the acts he will do. Go to him in three months, and ask him the result. It is not reality. It is Law, not Spirit; therefore the thing has failed. Therefore do I protest most earnestly against any attempt to carry this early closing movement by coercion. I protest against any thing like dictation to the master-tradesmen. I protest against any thing like an attempt at compulsion. It was said to me a few days ago, that this was a conspiracy against the masters. We repel that, in the name of the young men; we protest against it; we protest against every thing by which the masters may be held up to ridicule; and, with just as much indignation as I should protest against carrying the point by breaking windows in the street, I protest against any attempt to carry out the principle of exclusive dealing. I hold in my hands the report of a recent meeting in favour of exclusive dealing. It was with much regret that I read it.

I protest most strongly against this principle. In the first place, because it makes that prominent which ought to be subordinate. It is quite sufficient ground for dealing with a tradesman, that he is moral, that his wares are good; but when we take a ground such as this, that though he be a moral and good man, and sells goods better than his neighbours, because he does not choose to do what we do, we will not deal with him, we make that prominent which ought to be subordinate. Again, I protest against it because it is illiberal. There are men who hold—I believe mistakenly—that such a measure as this of Early Closing would be injurious to the young men and to society. We believe they are wrong, but it is their opinion; and I ask on what possible ground men can come forward and demand of us that we should deal exclusively, because a man does not hold our views on the subject, and then complain of us if we deal exclusively with those who hold our own political, or our own ecclesiastical views?

And now, to pass briefly to the remainder of what I have to say. All at present shows a difficulty; but nothing which is impracticable. Let it be clearly understood that in all those difficulties there is not one that *ought* to stand in the way of Early Closing; and I have a pleasure in proposing this resolution, because the language it uses is the language, not of coercion, nor of dictation, but of recommendation. It pledges us to recommend to all tradesmen the adoption of eight o'clock as the hour of closing. There are master tradesmen who do their duty by their assistants. There are some who look on their young men as objects committed by God to their charge, and desire to treat them as their children. And there are master tradesmen, who open for their young men rooms, and have lectures, and all kinds of instruction. Let us have but a hundred such masters, and the whole question of Early Closing is safe.

It is possible and practicable to force this question on the attention of the community. We pledge ourselves in this resolution to do all we can to promote so desirable an object, by making all purchases before the evening, and requesting the heads of establishments to do the same. Let us not pledge ourselves in a moment of enthusiasm. When the blood burns, we know how prodigally the tongue vows. It is easy in enthusiastic moments to make a pledge; but let us pledge ourselves, to endeavour to understand the immense importance of this subject, and to act out our convictions fully and completely. Let us understand that there are higher aims than merely obtaining Early Closing. What we want is, not to get a stringent law to carry out our own principles, but to promote a pervading spirit of good feeling through all classes; in one word, to feel that "we are members one of another."

A SPEECH

Delivered at a Meeting of the Brighton District Association for Improving the Dwellings of the Industrious Classes, held at the Pavilion, Brighton, November 25, 1852.

The Rev. F. W. Robertson moved,—" That this meeting hears with satisfaction the success which has attended the establishment of the Brighton Branch of the Metropolitan Association for Improving the Dwellings of the Industrious Classes, and is of opinion that the extension of the undertaking will be the means of conferring more extensively essential benefit on the social and moral condition of the working classes of the town of Brighton; and that such extension will be more effectually promoted by obtaining an increase in the number of shares, which it pledges itself to use its best exertions to effect."

It is to one sentence, alone, of this resolution that I shall direct a few observations: that in which we say that " this will be the means of conferring more extensively essential benefit on the social and moral condition of the working classes of the town of Brighton." The great object for which institutions, such as this, are established, is to procure for the working classes a "*Home*." To explain the meaning of this word is unnecessary; before an English audience it is superfluous. There is not one present to-day who has not been, even from childhood, familiar with all those sacred associations which God has thrown in such profusion around the precincts of Home; but to the great majority of the poor in this country, there is no such thing as Home. We dare not, cannot say, that those two small rooms in which a whole family are huddled up together; those two rooms which serve for kitchen, sleeping-room, parlour, and for every thing; in which there are no conveniences and no comforts, and in which, when a man or a child may be dying, he would be disturbed by the necessary noise and bustle of the family,—we dare not, except in mockery, call that, in a Christian land, a "*Home*."

Yet we too often ignore this condition of the poor man's dwelling, and hence arise many practical fallacies. I will mention but one: the mistake with respect to the possibility of the poor man spending the Lord's-day as he should. This subject has occupied much attention in this country. There has been a project recently set on foot by a large number of philanthropists, and a large number of speculators, in different parts of the country, to establish edifices or buildings in which the poor shall have recreation, pleasure, and instruction; and some of these, one especially, the importance of which overrides all the others, it has been proposed to open on the Lord's-day, and that too with the sanction of the Government. This has been met by a very large proportion of the religious inhabitants of this country with great dismay and indignation. It has appeared to them that this is a desecration of the Lord's-day, a breaking of the covenant between God and his people. They have drawn most touching pictures of the poor man spending his Sabbath evenings surrounded by his family, and with the Bible open before him. I am not about to pronounce any opinion with respect to the view entertained among religious people on this subject. There are two views entertained on this question, and both these ought, in all Christian consistency, to be allowed to those who hold them. Some believe that the Sabbath, the Jewish Sabbath, if not in its integrity and strictness, at all events with a certain degree of modified strictness, accordant with the superior genius of Christianity, should be observed. Some, on the other hand, believe that the Jewish Sabbath is altogether abrogated; that the Lord's-day is not the same thing; that it did not arise out of it, nor was it a transfer of one day to another, but that what has succeeded the Jewish Sabbath is not what we call the Lord's-day; that it is not one day alone that the Christian is to observe, but a grander, larger, more spiritual day, the day of the whole life, the sanctification of the whole life of man, to be yielded to God, as purchased by Christ. With respect to the truth of these two conflicting opinions, we have nothing, at present, to do. All we have to consider is, how far we can with any consistency agree upon this point. We are all agreed on this, that the most blessed institution which has descended to us from our forefathers is the Christian Lord's-day. All, I believe, are agreed in this: that it is deeply rooted as an institution in the necessities of our human nature; and that to give up the Lord's-day, merely to the physical or intellectual needs of man will be utterly insufficient, and that the higher and truer half of man, that which makes him a spiritual creature, being uncared for, the Sabbath will be but a very imperfect day of rest. We are all agreed also, in an earnest resolve to set our faces against those views, now so common, which identify the Christianizing of the population with the humanizing of the population. We believe that to humanize is one thing; that to Christianize is another thing. We believe that pictures, statues, music, æsthetics, tropical plants, and all the other contents and adjuncts of these places, valuable as they are in humanizing, are utterly insufficient to produce the Christianity of the Cross. We are all agreed in believing that there is a distinction between æsthetics and religious worship, between the worship of the Beautiful and the worship of Holiness. We are, therefore, all agreed in an earnest desire that, among all classes of the country, there should be a more religious, pure, and holy observance of the Lord's-day. But now, let me ask the question, With what consistency can we demand of the poor man that he shall have no recreation of an out-doors kind, if we have done nothing to provide for him a *home* within doors, wherein to spend the Christian Sabbath?

It was only yesterday that I conversed with an intelligent working man in this town, and the man expressed in very striking language the bitter indignation which was felt by his class towards those who were, as he said, in a bigoted way endeavouring to rob them of their Sabbath. I trust that I convinced him, I tried at all events with all my heart to convince him, that it was not bigotry in those who tried to take from the working men their Sabbath; but I am not sure that I convinced the man that there was not great ignorance on the part of those persons, with regard to the necessities of the poor. It seems, therefore, that the only true and proper answer we can make to the poor man, when he expresses indignation at being robbed of his out-door Sabbath, is by an institution such as this, which would give him a home wherein to spend an in-door Sabbath. Every institution of this kind seems to tell of a new era in the Human Race and of the progress of civilization. What is the true characteristic of the present age? It is a disposition to acknowledge the importance and the value of that which appears to be small and insignificant. When Mr. Wordsworth announced this as the great truth and the great principle of all the poetry of life, he was met with a universal shout of laughter; but the spirit of the remark has since permeated all society, and all our literature. It is the characteristic of the age—it is the characteristic of its literature. The most popular and the most vigorous of the writers of this day arose first to eminence by drawing the attention of the country to the modes of thinking, the feeling, the living, and even the slang of the lower classes; and that book which has occupied, and is still occupying the attention both of Europe and America,*—to what is owing its singular power, but to the thrilling interest it has thrown around the thought, that in the negro himself there is a common humanity with our own—in the lowest of the species something that agrees even with the highest! It must be an era marking a changed state of things, when princes and nobles, instead of occupying their time with battles and tournaments, are occupied with subjects such as Improving the Dwellings of the Poor, and the construction of Baths and Wash-houses. This, I think, must prove that we have arrived at a state of things in which the smallest, the minutest atoms of the species become of importance; when members of the Government are absolutely not ashamed to give lectures, and to enlighten the people on the necessity of drainage and sanitary regulations—surely this is significant. And in all this, we have, I think, the very genius and spirit of Christianity; we have that which, 1800 years ago, was declared when an Apostle told us, "Nay, more, those members of the body which seem to be more feeble are necessary; and those members of the body which we think to be less honourable, upon these we bestow more abundant honour."

In that book to which I have already adverted,

* "Uncle Tom's Cabin."

there is an incident related which struck me as it were with a flush of surprise, because it brought a well-known and little thought-of passage of Scripture under notice with new associations. It is that in which two adults are represented as gazing on the play of two young children. One of the children was a female slave; the other, the daughter of the lady of the mansion. Of the adults, one was a man whose feelings, as is but too commonly the case, were far beyond his attainments, his aspirations beyond his will. He had consequently sunk down into that state of mere sentimentalism, which is inseparably connected with thinking well and not doing well, and he is represented as contented with, from time to time, an indignant and sarcastic expression on the inconsistency of those around him. The other was a lady whose whole life had been spent in the acquisition of maxims, but who had not been able to live deeply in the spirit of those maxims. These children were at play, and one was seen to throw her arms around the other; and that other, who had evaded all attempts to soften, or to tame, was melted by the tenderness of her white sister; and an expression burst from the lips of the lady to the effect, that *now* she understood the deep meaning and spirit there was in the passage of Scripture, "He laid his hands upon them, and healed them." She had up to this time been uttering maxims with regard to the equality of the human race; but she had not "*laid her hands*" upon the negroes. I do not say but that this is fanciful; yet it strikes at the deep root of it all, for the great difference between His love of the human race and ours, the great difference in the way He stated the Brotherhood of the Race is this, that His was real, and true, and deep, and full of kindly sympathy. It was not standing apart from them; but mixing with them, and being one with them; and therefore it is, that what we are *now* to do is, to put *our* hands on our fellow-men, and touch the littleness and vulgarities of their daily life. It is just that which this institution desires to do, in building for them a Home. It has long appeared to me that Christianity is a true medium between those two opposite extremes, Spiritualism and Socialism. The spiritualist maintains that man may make his circumstances, and so it takes no account whatsoever of the circumstances by which the man may be surrounded; it believes that the Spirit, which is of God, may rise above those circumstances. On the other hand, it is a great maxim of Socialism that circumstances make the man. And so, the very author of Socialism tells us that, if we have efficient laws and altered Social regulations, we shall have true and right men; and if we will but take away all the temptations to vice, we shall have no vice. These are the two extreme systems; Christianity does not steer the *via media* between these two extremes—no *truth* does. Christianity states the truth, by stating both extremes. It is the spirit of Christianity, that man makes his circumstances, and, besides, that the circumstances make the man. The Scriptures, interested principally with our spiritual nature, are also interested with our physical nature; and the Redeemer of the soul is declared to be the Saviour also of the body. It appears to me that the grand consummation, for which all are waiting, the Kingdom of Christ set up on earth, never can be established till we have reached this conviction; and all the outer and inner life must work together, until we have done all that in us lies, not only to preach and teach the truth, but to take away the hindrances which stand in the way of truth. And what is the life of the poor man in his cottage?

Before a mixed audience, I cannot go deeply into the details of this. I have seen a family of nine, father and mother, grown-up sons and daughters, with but one sleeping-room, and in that sleeping-room only two beds. I will not go into the result; before a Christian assembly they are not to be named. But what is Purity, what is Modesty, what is the Christian Gospel preached to such a family as that? It may appear to some, that to have gone into all these large principles is something like magniloquence; for, after all, when we speak of what we have done, we have only built apartments for ten families and seven single persons. But the rest is to come; and it is a great thing to have established a standard, to have set up before our poorer brethren a specimen of a higher and better mode of living. Political economists say, the evil of the country is over-population consequent on improvident marriages. This is partly true, but their remedy is insufficient. There is no difficulty in preventing improvident marriages among the upper classes; and for this reason—they know what comfort is—and they will not, except there is very small self-control, marry and sink in the scale of society. But the poor man often feels that he can sink no lower. Why then, he might ask himself, should I not marry? And when this morning I saw the Building in Church Street, with every window curtained, and the whole aspect so different from the buildings around, the thought suggested itself to my mind, and it must also have suggested itself to the minds of those who accompanied me,—It is impossible that those who live in this locality, and look at this building, should be satisfied with the state in which they are now living. They will aspire to higher things. We are bound, every one of us, to pledge ourselves to use our best exertions to effect the prosperity of such an Institution as this Society for improving the Dwellings of the Labouring Classes.

A SPEECH

In reply to an Address presented to him by One Hundred Young Men of his Congregation, at the Town Hall, Brighton, April 20, 1852.

Mr. Chairman and Gentlemen,—I should be guilty of affectation if I were to disguise the satisfaction and deep gratefulness which I feel for the Address which you have just presented me. No one can feel more deeply than I do, the deficiencies, the faults, the worthlessness of the ministry of which you have spoken so kindly and so warmly. Whatever eyes have scanned those deficiencies, I will answer for it that none have scanned them so severely as my own. Others may have detected its faults more keenly, no one has felt them as bitterly as I have. And yet, for all this, I shall not for one moment disguise my belief that much of what has been said to-night is true. We have not come here to bandy compliments with one another. You have not come to flatter me; and I have not come, with any affected coyness, to pretend to disclaim your flattery, in order that it may be repeated. You have told me, in the frank spirit of Englishmen, that my ministry has done you good. Frankly, as an Englishman, I tell you with all my heart, I do believe it. I know that there are men who once wandered in darkness and doubt, and could find no light, who have now found an anchor, and a rock, and resting-place. I know that there are men who were feeling bitterly and angrily, what seemed to them the unfair differences of society, who now regard them in a gentler, more humble, and more tender spirit. I know that there are rich who have been led to feel more generously towards the poor. I know that there are poor who have been taught to feel more truly, and more fairly towards the rich. I *believe*—for on such a point *God* can only *know*—that there are men who have been induced to place before themselves a higher standard, and perhaps I may venture to add, have conformed their lives more truly to that standard. I dare not hide my belief in this. I am deeply grateful in being able to say that, if my ministry were to close to-morrow it would not have been, in this town at least, altogether a failure. There is no vanity in saying this. A man must be strangely constituted indeed if he can say such things, and not feel deeply humbled in remembering what that instrument is, how weak, how frail, how feeble, by which the work is done. I desire to feel this evening far less the honour that may have been done to myself, than the opportunity that is given to us for meeting together in Christian union and brotherhood. We are met here to-night, a minister of the Church of England, a minister of the Gospel of Jesus Christ, invited by young men, of that age at which it is generally supposed that the hot blood of youth incapacitates, or indisposes them towards religion. We are met here, many of those around me of the richer classes of society, invited by those who are in a humbler and far poorer class, and is it possible for me to see in a picture such as this, merely the prominent object of myself? Is it possible for me, as a Christian, to see any thing in this—almost any thing—except a foretaste of better and happier times? A pledge of a coming time, when that shall be realized, of which that which we now see is but the representation; like the ancient *agapæ*, or feasts of charity, in which the Corinthian churches, and many other churches, exhibited before the world the blessed fact of a Church, and of a Brotherhood existing here on earth. These signatures, which are appended to this

Address you have given me, will be to me, I trust, in future times, in many a dark hour, a consolation and encouragement. For if I have been liable—and what public man has not—to have at times, and in certain quarters, my words misrepresented, my motives misconstrued, the whole aim and object of my teaching utterly perverted—unintentionally, I am sure—yet surely—surely—there is a rich recompense in the warm and affectionate professions of respect which you have made to me this night. Surely there is abundant overpayment, in the affectionate regard with which I have been met in Brighton, in so many personal attachments, some of the kindest and warmest of those friends being now around me, for whose presence here this evening, I have to thank your graceful and touching courtesy. My young friends—my dear brethren—I had meant to say more—I had intended to briefly sketch the principles of my public teaching; but I would far rather leave what Mr. Evans has said of it, knowing it as he does, to speak for itself. Far rather than that I should speak of my own principles, I would have the decisive testimony of that young man to reply to all the misconceptions and perversions that have been uttered of my work. His words shall answer for it, whether there is Rationalism or Socialism in my teaching.

A SPEECH

Delivered at the Town Hall, Brighton, November 14, 1850, at a Meeting held for the Purpose of Addressing the Queen in reference to the Attempt of the Pope of Rome to parcel England out into Ecclesiastical Dioceses under Cardinal Wiseman.

When I entered th s room, I had not the smallest intention of addressing the Meeting; but certain expressions which have been used since my arrival seem to make it necessary. However that may be, if this were simply a question between the Church of England and the Church of Rome—if it were merely a question of precedence between the Archbishop of Canterbury and Cardinal Wiseman, I should hold it purely superfluous to attend this meeting. As a member of the Church of England, certainly consistently, as every dissenter will acknowledge, I hold that the Bishop of Rome has been guilty of an act of schism. It was a principle of the early Church, that every church, every kingdom, is supreme in spiritual matters within itself, and that every bishop is vested with authority in his own diocese. So far as this goes we, the members, and especially the clergy, of the Church of England, have reason to consider ourselves aggrieved; but all that would be necessary for us to do in such a case is to do what we have done,—address our Bishop. We should be by no means justified in calling so large a meeting, of our fellow countrymen and fellow townsmen, a large mass of whom are not members of the Church of England, to address the Sovereign.

If this were merely a matter between Protestant and Roman Catholic in point of doctrine, I should feel that nothing more than a protest was necessary. I confess that it seems to me that to say "We are right and the Roman Catholics are wrong, and therefore the Roman Catholics may not proselytize because they are wrong, and we may because we are right;" is a *petitio principii*, a begging of the question, an assumption of the very thing in dispute. I acknowledge that I have but very small sympathy with those intolerant controversialists who imitate the Church of Rome in thundering out anathemas against their brother

Christians. I have small sympathy with those persons who are trying to arouse popular indignation against Romanism, by endeavouring to prove that the Pope of Rome is "The Man of Sin," and the Church of Rome a "Synagogue of Satan." Let there be proselytism by fair argument; let there be a fair field and no favour. Let them do what they can; and, in the name of God, we will do what we can. We do not fear Rome. Let them have fair play; we ask no more. For such questions as these, we do not require such meetings.

The ground on which I stand here, the reason on which I protest against this Papal Act, is the assumption of Infallibility which it contains. It is a claim by an individual man, or by a body of men, of a *right* to press on the consciences of mankind, *authoritatively*, opinions of their own. Whether that view be thundered from the Vatican, or be thundered from Exeter Hall, or come from the assumed infallibility of a private pulpit, be it Dissenting or Church of England, I believe it to be our bounden duty, as Protestants, to protest against it.

I stand forward on behalf of the right of private judgment. I would almost rather retract that expression; for the words "private judgment" have a proud sound. It seems to assume that private judgment *must* be right; that every man may judge what he will, and that, forsooth, having judged it, he, in the omnipotence of his individual judgment, must be right. I do not so understand it. A man has not a right to judge what he will; he may judge what is right; the right of private judgment is the right of judging the right. I retract the expression I used just now, and stand up on behalf of the Rights of Conscience,—not the right of man to have what conscience he will, but the right of conscience to control the man and demand allegiance to its decrees. I protest against the Popish claim for this reason,—that it is an assumption of man to dictate, in the forum of conscience, to his brother man.

There is something besides which I would rather not have said; and for that reason I entered this room intending not to say one word. There is an expression in that Address to which in committee I raised an objection. It is that where we call for the remedy which justice demands for the act that has been done. I know my brother ministers meant that they demand no pains and penalties, but merely require and wish that the titles should be ignored; and yet the expression is one from which, in all freedom, I felt myself shrink. I do not like to ask the interference of the Law; I do not like to ask or protection in such a matter; I do not like to seem to stand forward and demand that the titles of the Church of England should be preserved by forms of law—those of the Church of Rome ignored. There is something in this which appears to speak of fear and apprehension. In my heart of hearts, I have no apprehension of the progress of the Church of Rome. Let men say what they will; let them number up the chapels that have increased—I grant that there has been an increase; but what if it be that a few hundred ladies have been embroidering altar-cloths, and a few hundred of the aristocracy, unable to keep their own consciences, and not daring to go into the awful question, "What is truth?" have chosen, like children afraid of the dark, to go back to their mother's aprons, and throw themselves on Papal infallibility? What if a few, soft, sentimental clergymen have gone to Rome? What then, has *that* touched the great, clear, sturdy English heart? When once this question of Romanism, or Tractarianism, or semi-Romanism has been placed before the mass of the country, there has never been a moment of hesitation; it has been met by stern rejection. And, therefore, Mr. Chairman, acknowledging the rightful meaning of the words, and perfectly prepared to sign that memorial, I should rather have rejoiced if we had been contented with a simple protest.

A few words on the matter with which the last speaker concluded and I have done. It seems to me that he is under some misapprehension with respect to that expression—"spiritual supremacy." He objects to it, if I understand him, on the supposition that it gives to the Sovereign spiritual jurisdiction,—the right of doing spiritual acts. The Sovereign of England does no spiritual act whatsoever. She does not ordain ministers; she does *nothing* with regard to the administration of the sacraments; she does not create one single doctrine. There seems to be a certain misapprehension in respect of the very meaning of the ground on which this was originally proposed. The speaker dwelt much on the authority and rights of the people,—the supremacy of the people. He spoke of the people as the fountain source of all power, spiritually probably, as well as temporally. Is that gentleman aware that the great defender of this doctrine of royal supremacy in matters ecclesiastical—for that is the real meaning, here, of spiritual—did uphold that the people are the rightful sources of all spiritual authority? God has delegated to his church, to the mass of believers, a right to govern themselves according to Scripture and Truth, but as a matter of order, not in heaven, but here on earth, it became necessary for the country, that is, the Christian community at large,—for in those days the church was the country and the country the church,—that the country should delegate to one individual all its sovereignty; and the Sovereign now speaks spiritually, speaks ecclesiastically, only as the delegate and voice of the sovereign community of the Church of Christ.

www.ingramcontent.com/pod-product-compliance
Lightning Source LLC
LaVergne TN
LVHW010147110826
845151LV00002B/447

* 9 7 8 1 4 2 5 5 3 8 4 0 8 *